*terrain*

# *terrain*

## Ideas and Inspiration for
## Decorating the Home and Garden

———

Edited *by* Greg Lehmkuhl
and the gardeners of Terrain

Words *by* Caroline Lees

Principal photography *by* Isa Salazar

ARTISAN | NEW YORK

Library of Congress Cataloging-in-Publication Data

Names: Lehmkuhl, Greg, editor.
Title: Terrain : ideas and inspiration for decorating the home and garden /
    edited by Greg Lehmkuhl & the gardeners of Terrain ; words by Caroline Lees ;
    principal photography by Isa Salazar.
Description: New York, NY : Artisan, a division of Workman Publishing Co., Inc. [2018] |
    Includes index.
Identifiers: LCCN 2018023578 | ISBN 9781579658076 (hardcover : alk. paper)
Subjects: LCSH: Gardening—Pictorial works. | Interior decoration.
Classification: LCC SB450.98 .T47 2018 | DDC 635—dc23
LC record available at https://lccn.loc.gov/2018023578

Art direction and cover design by Danielle Palencar
Design by Justin Speers

Artisan books are available at special discounts when purchased in bulk for premiums and sales
promotions as well as for fund-raising or educational use. Special editions or book excerpts also can
be created to specification. For details, contact the Special Sales Director at the address below, or
send an e-mail to specialmarkets@workman.com.

For speaking engagements, contact speakersbureau@workman.com.

Published by Artisan
A division of Workman Publishing Co., Inc.
225 Varick Street
New York, NY 10014-4381
artisanbooks.com

Artisan is a registered trademark of Workman Publishing Co., Inc.

Published simultaneously in Canada by Thomas Allen & Son, Limited

Printed in China

First printing, September 2018

10 9 8 7 6 5 4 3 2 1

# Contents

# Putting Down Roots

Terrain began with a search for something new, a desire to turn away from the mass production that characterized American gardening at the start of the twenty-first century and establish a stronger, more honest connection with nature. With the support of lifelong plant lover and URBN founder Dick Hayne, along with the creative people who have shaped the URBN family of brands, we set out to establish a different kind of garden center, one that would celebrate the world of plants in all its beauty, diversity, and imperfection.

Our pursuit of a new perspective took us farther than we could have imagined. We traveled to places with long and rich histories of gardening, touring the renowned landscapes of English country homes, visiting German Christmas marketplaces piled high with fresh greens, and admiring the simple, refined ways Scandinavians bring the outdoors into their homes. At the end of our explorations, we returned invigorated and eager to combine these pockets of inspiration and tradition into a fresh approach for the American gardener. This mission was at the heart of our plans as the first Terrain store took shape, and—ten years later—it remains the driving force behind all we do.

Gardeners are generous people, eager to offer advice and ideas along with seeds and cuttings from their vegetable patches and flower beds. They especially love to share the unusual and unexpected—and so do we. The natural world contains beauty in countless forms, from the tender petals of spring and the rangy wildflowers of summer to the dried leaves of autumn and the bare branches of winter. Each of these elements can find a place in planters, vases, wreaths, garlands, and myriad other projects for indoors and out. In the pages that follow, we've gathered some of our favorite ways to bring the garden into every part of our lives. By offering them to a wider audience, we hope to reflect on all we've learned, spark a creative reconsideration of what the world outside has to offer, and inspire our community of gardeners to see nature in new ways.

—Greg Lehmkuhl

# Into the Garden

We opened the doors to Terrain at Styer's in 2008, our nursery filled with spring's brightest blooms and our minds overflowing with hopes and plans for the seasons ahead. The establishment of our flagship store was the happy result of a long search for a place to call our own. Though we considered every corner of the country when seeking the location for the first Terrain, the journey ultimately led us to our own backyard. Our discovery of John Franklin Styer's historic nursery just outside Philadelphia felt like a homecoming—we had found the perfect place for a space devoted to nature, to finding wonder in its whims and flaws and to introducing the beauty of plants into our customers' homes as well as their gardens. With a long-standing place in the world of gardening, this space would indelibly shape the spirit of our new venture.

Upon the opening of Terrain at Styer's, we were honored to become part of southeastern Pennsylvania's rich horticultural heritage; the region is famous for its noteworthy gardens, with Kennett Square's Longwood Gardens as its crown jewel. Within the city limits, gardens large and small flourish as well. Bartram's Garden holds the title of oldest botanical garden in America, Wyck offers a tiny jewel box

John Franklin Styer's nursery—which would eventually become Terrain at Styer's—traces its roots to 1875, when the farmer purchased eighty-five acres of land in Concordville, Pennsylvania. When Styer's grandson took over in 1924, the accomplished horticulturist transformed the roadside stand into a garden landmark featuring plants of all kinds—particularly peonies. His remarkable flowers became famous, and even served as the signature bloom at White House state dinners.

of heirloom roses, and a Japanese landscape materializes in West Fairmount Park at Shofuso. The Woodlands and the Highlands, Winterthur and Chanticleer, the Scott, Tyler, Morris, and Barnes Arboretums—this corner of Pennsylvania is a plant lover's wonderland, and it has done much to determine who we are today. We also found ourselves surrounded by a collective of creative people—our designers, the growers and makers who became our partners, and above all, our customers—who joined with us in a deep-seated love of all nature has to offer for our homes, gardens, and spirits.

The rich history of our region paired with the enthusiasm of the community around us has shaped our ethos and placed Terrain at the intersection of nature and design. It has also inspired us to ask some fundamental questions: How can we translate all that we've learned into a new approach to gardening? How can we bring to light the subtle and surprising moments of beauty in nature? How can we shape a lifestyle lived outdoors and in?

This book includes some of our best answers to these questions: inventive ideas and designs for container plantings, wreaths, arrangements, and holiday décor that forge a connection between the natural world and our living spaces. Interspersed with these sections are our seasonal spotlights, featuring visits to farms and gardens we admire and explorations of seasonal traditions.

We've grown a lot in the ten years since we chose Styer's nursery as our first home, but a few things remain the same. We're constantly inspired by nature, informed by the traditions of gardeners before us, and in search of fresh ways to decorate with plants and invite the garden into every space. We see the possibilities of the outside world in each season and embrace its imperfections as signs of constant growth and change.

We encourage you to explore the ideas in the pages that follow with your own garden in mind, and to adapt them with the materials that can be found outside your door. As Terrain marks its first decade, we're thrilled to share our perspective from the garden. We invite you to join us in a celebration of every season, every stem, and every way to bring nature home. Let's go outside.

# Spotlight on Spring

*emergence & ephemera*

The year's first season, like a garden's bounty, arrives in fits and starts. Fresh shoots peek through soil. Bees hastily buzz, collecting nectar for their burgeoning hives. Fragrant blossoms festoon the branches of fruit trees, and bulbs break ground, anticipating vibrant arrangements that will top the table at springtime gatherings. These tiny, fleeting signs mark the end of hibernation, in both nature and ourselves. It is the moment to head outdoors and witness the work in progress, plant seeds of future growth, or simply pause to relish the earth's renewal.

With so much new life, it's no wonder that spring is a season of celebration, from Easter to Mother's Day. Beyond those occasions, spring is a celebration in itself—of the garden's most colorful arrivals and a return to life outside. The pages that follow explore the season's transitory and transcendent pleasures.

## Day Trip
# Hortulus Farm Springs to Life

One of Pennsylvania's secret treasures, Hortulus Farm Garden and Nursery is tucked into the bucolic landscape of Bucks County, an hour outside of Philadelphia. An original William Penn land grant, the property is anchored by an eighteenth-century stone house and a number of historic farm buildings, many still home to a menagerie of animals. Three hundred acres were granted to the original owner, Isaiah Warner, in 1690, but the farm dwindled to just fifteen acres in the wake of the Great Depression. In 1980, Hortulus was purchased by famed garden and event designer Renny Reynolds and garden author Jack Staub, who have developed the estate into one of Pennsylvania's most acclaimed gardens.

Renny and Jack have worked tirelessly to restore the farm, acquiring one hundred of its original three hundred acres. Today, Hortulus is home to twenty-four formal gardens, plus a specialty nursery for rare plants and native perennials. A grand birch allée welcomes visitors to the property, leading through fern glades and deep woods to a peaceful pond complete with gliding black

swans and a fairy-tale pavilion. Near the original farmhouse, kitchen gardens, herbs, and fruit trees flourish alongside nineteenth-century barns. Beyond the house, a circular swimming pool is surrounded by a Mediterranean garden, crab apple orchard, and arboretum filled with specimen trees.

Spring is an especially beautiful time at Hortulus, as border gardens, lawns, and woodlands overflow with more than two hundred thousand flowers, including narcissus, bluebells, dogwoods, and Delaware Valley white azaleas. At every turn, another striking vista awaits visitors, making for a full and wonderful day of exploration.

# Container Plantings

In Ancient Greece, women celebrated Adonia—an annual festival to mourn the death of the god Adonis—by planting container gardens. In shallow baskets and bowls, they sowed quick-germinating seeds like wheat, barley, and lettuce, then carried these diminutive gardens to the rooftops. After eight days of careful tending, they tossed their newly sprouted plants—pots and all—into the ocean. These ancient "gardens of Adonis" capture the dual nature of container gardens: their enduring presence in landscapes through the ages and the ephemeral beauty of their living contents.

Though the concept of container gardening has existed for thousands of years, the majority of plants sold in a nursery in decades past were destined for placement in a garden bed or border. Gardeners may have tended a small collection of potted plants—a window box, a single pot on the doorstep—but larger plantings reigned supreme. Recently, however, the popularity of container gardens has increased dramatically as gardeners have come to embrace the variety and adaptability of planters both indoors and out.

Whether in the smallest corner of a hidden path or the grandest entryway, planters expand the landscape beyond its natural borders. They offer opportunities to experiment, to embrace the fleeting splendor of each season, and to plant with a creativity that exceeds the limited confines of the vessel itself. The growing prevalence of containers also reflects changes in the way we live. In urban and rural communities alike, outdoor living and entertaining have become a priority. City dwellers brighten their balconies with small-scale gardens, while expansive patios are transformed into open-air rooms, where planters provide accent pieces to soften hardscapes and enhance outdoor furnishings. And container gardens are well suited to our busy lifestyles, offering a "quick fix" for those who want to get their hands dirty and create something lovely without the time investment of a full-scale garden.

This exploration of container gardens begins with planting advice that provides the backbone for the designs that follow, including high-style installations like green walls and living archways and seasonal statements that showcase the most remarkable specimens at every point in the year. These miniature gardens are approachable, adaptable, and above all else, beautiful.

PREVIOUS PAGES: Late-summer blooms provide a riot of saturated color atop a textured urn. Dahlias, coleus, red Russian kale, and *Penstemon* 'Husker Red' create a rich burgundy palette, offset by the vivid greens of *Dichondra* and little bluestem (*Schizachyrium scoparium*).

OPPOSITE: In times of seasonal transition, empty vessels can serve as sculptural stand-ins for their fully planted counterparts. This look is best suited to pieces with a unique silhouette, a noteworthy finish, or intricate detailing.

# 1

*Embrace the Ephemeral*

# Our Planting Philosophy

With countless plants, vessels, and styles available to mix and match, every planter is a personalized creation, designed to suit a specific location, season, and aesthetic. The beauty of container gardening lies in its potential for reinvention; a single vessel can be transformed over and over with new plants and a fresh perspective. Through years of garden experimentation, however, we've identified a few guiding principles we keep in mind for every container planting. From the perfect mix of high and low elements to the addition of foraged finds, these are the key ingredients for a well-planted container that offers layers of complexity and visual interest. Pair the guidance in the following pages with another piece of advice, from beloved British gardener Christopher Lloyd: "The great thing is not to be timid in your gardening, whether it's colours, shapes, juxtapositions or the contents themselves. Splash around and enjoy yourself."

# Contrast High-Low Style

A successful container garden often begins with the meeting of opposites, using disparate elements to create a high-low effect. The juxtaposition of textures is central to many high-low displays; pairing a polished vessel with wild, natural plants keeps a container from feeling too fussy. A formal planter (think Grecian urn or Wedgwood jardiniere) plays perfect counterpoint to an informal planting—cascades of grass, gnarled branches, spills of saturated blooms. By challenging expectations of traditional vessel-plant combinations, these contrasting containers encourage closer observation and bring a playful spirit to the garden.

The formal shape of a rusted wire urn finds equilibrium in a humble planting of overgrown chives (*Allium schoenoprasum*). A tangled liner of pine straw grounds the high-low look.

Ornamental grasses put on a four-season show: they're sturdy enough to offer impactful texture and movement from spring through winter. Pair an overflowing collection of shaggy, plumelike grasses with a weighty urn for a playful study in high-low contrast.

## Ornamental Grasses

Offering myriad benefits for creating planters with romantically untamed silhouettes, the grasses below are our favorites for color, texture, height, and shade tolerance.

### COLOR

 **Blue grama grass (*Bouteloua gracilis* 'Blonde Ambition')**: This small-scale specimen offers ample garden interest, with blue-gray leaves, chartreuse flowers, and long-lasting seed heads in pale gold.

 **Pink muhly grass (*Muhlenbergia capillaris*)**: The perennial pink muhly grass is beloved for its cloudlike inflorescences in eye-catching fuchsia.

 **Little bluestem (*Schizachyrium scoparium*)**: This prairie native is an outstanding autumn ornamental thanks to late-season foliage in bronze and orange.

 **Ruby grass (*Melinis nerviglumis* 'Pink Crystals')**: Native to Africa, this tropical favorite is prized for its bright pink summer flowers, which fade to white in autumn.

### TEXTURE

 **Inland sea oats (*Chasmanthium latifolium*)**: This clump-forming grass is highly textured thanks to its drooping, oatlike seed heads.

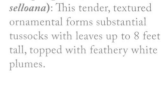 **Pampas grass (*Cortaderia selloana*)**: This tender, textured ornamental forms substantial tussocks with leaves up to 8 feet tall, topped with feathery white plumes.

 **Mexican feather grass (*Nassella tenuissima*)**: So named for its delicate, threadlike blades that wave in the wind, this silky grass introduces dramatic texture to any planting.

 **Quaking grass (*Briza media*)**: The tufted quacking grass's dramatic dangling seed heads move in even the slightest breeze.

### HEIGHT

 **Giant reed grass (*Arundo donax* 'Peppermint Stick')**: This deer-resistant Mediterranean native reaches up to 12 feet tall, with blades striped in green and white.

 **Switchgrass (*Panicum virgatum* 'Shenandoah')**: A hardy prairie dweller, switchgrass grows up to 6 feet tall with airy clouds of pink flowers in midsummer.

### SHADE TOLERANCE

 **Japanese forest grass (*Hakonechloa macra* 'Aureola')**: This Japanese native tolerates all but the deepest shade and features gracefully curved leaves variegated in green and gold.

 **Tufted hair grass (*Deschampsia cespitosa*)**: Tolerant of moderate shade, this cool-season ornamental forms low, dense tussocks of narrow blades.

# Celebrate Wild & Imperfect Forms

While well-manicured specimens in sleek vessels have a tidy appeal, a less polished planting showcases the unpredictable beauty of the natural world. A planter that celebrates imperfection—from overgrown stems to weathered materials—embraces the ever-changing nature of the garden itself. Allow flowers to spill over the sides of a planting, let grasses go to seed in dramatic plumes, and welcome the marks of weather on metal, wood, and stone vessels. In spotlighting these wild forms rather than fighting against them, a planter truly becomes a miniature reflection of the landscape.

The beauty of imperfection is nowhere more apparent than in a meadow-inspired container garden. Rangy grasses and riotous blooms capture the bounty of a mature meadow, letting nature take over while offering a plethora of tiny details to invite closer study. The diverse textures, bold scale, and rich colors of a meadow garden make for a planter that feels exceptionally lush and full, without the constraints of meticulous planning and pruning.

OPPOSITE: Flushed with spring blooms, a dappled willow (*Salix integra* 'Hakuro-nishiki') serves as an unexpectedly elegant centerpiece for a planter of aged wood and rusted iron. The unpretentious air of the vessel inspires a meadow-style underplanting (see page 83), filled with an early mix of flowering arugula, gypsophila, chocolate cosmos, and trailing bougainvillea, plus *Salvia* 'Hot Lips' and pink evening primrose (*Oenothera speciosa*) to echo the soft blush tones of the willow.

# Find Beauty in Your Backyard

When seeking an impactful accent for a planted vessel, head into the wild. Worn by the elements, branches are particularly well suited to container plantings, where they can serve as organic sculptures, yielding unexpected riches of structure, texture, and color. Their striking size and untamed forms enliven even the simplest plantings, ramping up scale, adding drama, and serving as the focal point for a planter. Nearly any branch with a unique shape can serve as an accent piece, but here are a few of our favorites.

**FRUIT TREES:** Thanks to their naturally ornate forms, the branches and trunks of apple, pear, and peach trees are ideal for plantings that demand an intricate shape. Limbs and trunks can often be sourced from orchards, where less productive trees are removed to make way for new plantings.

**DRIFTWOOD:** Naturally patinated by exposure to salt water, driftwood's smooth texture and cool gray coloration lend themselves to contemporary plantings.

**GHOSTWOOD:** Ghostwood is made by sandblasting the twisting branches of manzanita (*Arctostaphylos*), an evergreen shrub found in chaparral plant communities of the American West and Mexico. Sandblasting reveals the stark beauty of the bone-white wood beneath the manzanita's reddish bark.

**GRAPEVINE TRUNK:** While dried grapevines are a common material for decorating and wreath construction, their trunks' warped, knobby shapes also offer sculptural appeal for a planting. Like fruit trees, they can be sourced from growers who are removing unproductive plants.

**BITTERSWEET:** For a wild and wiry look, lengths of American bittersweet vine (*Celastrus scandens*) can be woven into a planting alongside foraged branches. This low-growing vine, most often found along the ground or circling trees, is best foraged in autumn or winter, when its appeal is heightened by clusters of showy red berries. (Learn to spot the difference between American and invasive Oriental bittersweet on page 150.)

A nest of foraged branches and vines frames an urn of densely planted sedges (*Carex*) and dianthus. Woven throughout the grasses, they create waves that mirror the rippling rim of the vessel.

# 2

*Planters*

# Materials & Making

In eighteenth-century Europe, when gardening evolved from an aristocratic pursuit to a popular pastime, planters came in two primary forms: one ornamental, the other utilitarian. Elegant urns, with their graceful curves and ornate bases, were decidedly decorative, whether they were lining estate walkways or surveying groomed gardens. At the opposite end of the spectrum lay common hand-thrown flowerpots, which were used to transport plants from far-flung locales and served as temporary homes for sprouting seeds and propagation.

Conventional roles have since relaxed. Today, traditional urns and simple pots are equally esteemed for their respective forms and functions, and they often reside alongside ceramic, wood, metal, and salvaged vessels in wildly varied silhouettes. In the following pages, we'll survey the world of contemporary planters with guides to classic and modern container styles, overviews of popular materials and silhouettes, and practical advice for planting and design.

# A Guide to Container Materials

When choosing outdoor planters, materials are paramount. The chart below takes a closer look at the most popular options, with manufacturing information, special features, and ratings for winter weather.

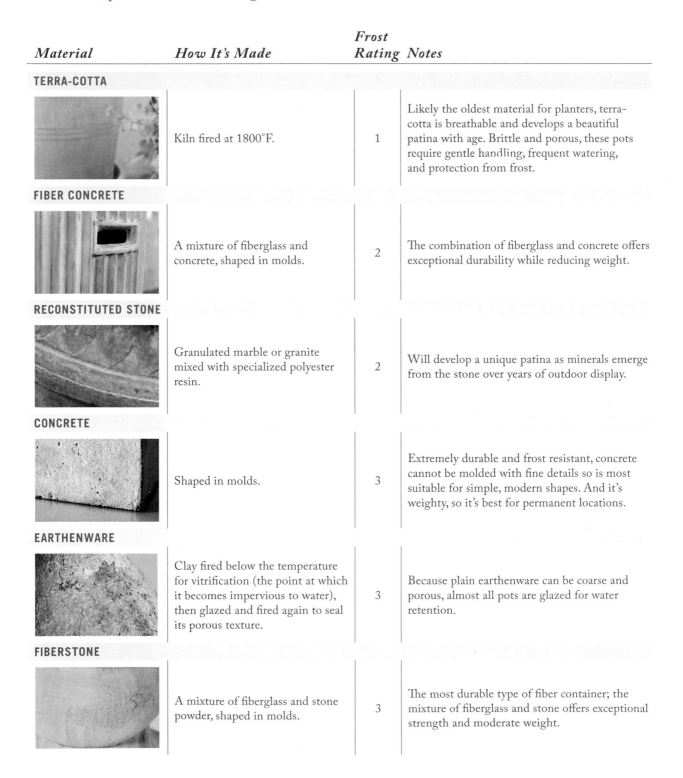

| Material | How It's Made | Frost Rating | Notes |
|---|---|---|---|
| **TERRA-COTTA** | Kiln fired at 1800°F. | 1 | Likely the oldest material for planters, terracotta is breathable and develops a beautiful patina with age. Brittle and porous, these pots require gentle handling, frequent watering, and protection from frost. |
| **FIBER CONCRETE** | A mixture of fiberglass and concrete, shaped in molds. | 2 | The combination of fiberglass and concrete offers exceptional durability while reducing weight. |
| **RECONSTITUTED STONE** | Granulated marble or granite mixed with specialized polyester resin. | 2 | Will develop a unique patina as minerals emerge from the stone over years of outdoor display. |
| **CONCRETE** | Shaped in molds. | 3 | Extremely durable and frost resistant, concrete cannot be molded with fine details so is most suitable for simple, modern shapes. And it's weighty, so it's best for permanent locations. |
| **EARTHENWARE** | Clay fired below the temperature for vitrification (the point at which it becomes impervious to water), then glazed and fired again to seal its porous texture. | 3 | Because plain earthenware can be coarse and porous, almost all pots are glazed for water retention. |
| **FIBERSTONE** | A mixture of fiberglass and stone powder, shaped in molds. | 3 | The most durable type of fiber container; the mixture of fiberglass and stone offers exceptional strength and moderate weight. |

| Material | How It's Made | Frost Rating | Notes |
|---|---|---|---|
| **HYPERTUFA** | A blend of peat moss, vermiculite/perlite, and cement, shaped in a mold. | 3 | A lightweight alternative to natural stone, hypertufa is weather resistant and pairs well with many landscape materials. Blends made with larger amounts of peat moss may be more vulnerable to frost. |
| **STONEWARE** | High-fired at 1800°F–2400°F. | 3 | High firing temperatures vitrify the clay, making it exceptionally strong and impervious to water. Most stoneware planters are glazed. |
| **ALL-WEATHER WICKER** | Made from furniture-grade synthetic wicker. | 4 | All-weather wicker is UV resistant and completely freezeproof. |
| **GALVANIZED STEEL** | Steel dipped into molten zinc, which chemically bonds to the iron in the steel. | 4 | The galvanized finish forms an impermeable seal, which is weatherproof and will not break down over time. |
| **METAL** | Hanging baskets and wall-mounted containers are made from treated wire. Cast iron is shaped in a mold from liquid iron. Antique and repurposed options include lead, bronze, copper, and brass. | 4 | Untreated metal rusts over time; clean and seal it to preserve the original finish. Coat the interior of copper and brass vessels with bituminous paint before planting. |
| **WOOD** | Teak and hardwoods should be sustainably grown in managed forests, or reclaimed. Softer woods should be treated with a nontoxic preservative. | 4 | Thick wood planters provide excellent heat insulation. When selecting them, inspect for flaws and choose designs with rustproof screws rather than nails. |

## FROST RATINGS

1: Suitable for outdoor use only when the weather is warm. Store indoors when freezing temperatures may occur.

2: For best longevity, empty and place upside down on boards or pot feet if stored outdoors during the winter months.

3: Likely to survive frost even when planted. Be sure water can drain from the planter to avoid freeze and thaw. Store indoors in extreme cold.

4: Frostproof and able to withstand most winter conditions without special care.

# A Guide to Container Silhouettes

The growing popularity of container gardens has prompted an explosion of planter silhouettes. The modern gardener's repertoire extends from classical urns to sleek bowls and angular cubes with contemporary flair. Each shape is suited for different plants; some containers offer ample soil surface area and volume for large, deep-rooted specimens, while others require shallow roots and diligent watering. Keep these practical concerns in mind, then seek visual harmony between plant and vessel: a simply tapered flowerpot for cheerful spring bulbs, a substantial cube planter for a deep-rooted tree, or a tall column for spilling vines. Beyond these considerations, personal style can lead the way.

| CLASSIC | FOOTED | BASKET | HANDLED |

**TAPER:** Available in myriad sizes and materials, the taper is one of the most popular planter styles. Round, square, and rectangular shapes are common, all defined by sloping sides. Most taper planters offer moderate to large soil surface area.

| WATER | EGG | DOLLY | MINIMAL |

**JAR:** These egg- or barrel-shaped planters are similar to the taper but possess a curved silhouette that creates a welcoming and informal appearance. Most offer moderate to large soil surface area. Those with mouths that are narrower than their body width, however, are best suited for planting a single specimen.

| CLASSIC | CUBE | LATTICE | FRAME |

**STRAIGHT-SIDED:** Due to their abundant soil volume and surface area, straight-sided planters are a good choice for cultivating larger specimens, including trees. Their stately shapes are ideal for displays of multiples, such as a symmetrical pair framing an entryway or a line of many dividing two outdoor areas.

| ABSTRACT | DISH | MINIMAL | PEDESTAL |

**BOWL:** Bowls offer a large soil surface area but lack depth, so they're best matched with plants that have a shallow root structure, such as succulents and alpine specimens. Shallow bowls are ideal for display atop a pedestal, along the edge of a staircase, or on a table.

| CLASSIC | BASKET | FLUTED | LOW |

**URN:** Elegant and often intricately shaped, urns are an elevated option for stylish plantings. Most urns, however, offer limited soil volume, making them a poor choice for deep-rooted plants or specimens that need lots of water. During the summer months, be sure to water urns frequently for optimal plant health.

| CLASSIC | FULL-LENGTH | CRISSCROSS | MINIMAL |

**TROUGH:** Ranging from sleek centerpieces to antique vessels, troughs are defined by their rectangular shape. Because most troughs are meant to be placed on another surface, their scale is generally small, as is their soil capacity. Design trough plantings with repetition down the length of the vessel to showcase your favorite plants.

# Our Favorite Planter Styles

Thousands of years ago, potters in Asia wrapped clay vessels in linen and let them slowly dry before firing, lending each piece an irregular, exquisitely aged finish. Centuries later, the beauty of imperfection continues to guide classical container style while modern container gardens are rooted in the unexpected, departing from tradition in material, shape, and placement.

1 | **HANGING BASKETS:** Hanging baskets have been a fixture on summer porches for decades, but contemporary shapes—like these sleek zinc spheres—refresh this classic style. Baskets take the garden to eye level and above, and their airy nature spotlights trailing plants with unusual shapes (find a guide to trailing plants on page 77).

2 | **LOW BOWLS:** Sleek and shapely, shallow bowls boast ample space to highlight a low-profile planting. Placed on the ground, they also offer a rare overhead view of the plants within.

3 | **REPURPOSED OBJECTS:** Found and renewed vessels like these antique English dolly tubs once used to hand-wash clothing bring a storied provenance to the garden.

4 | **AGED METAL:** Galvanized containers can withstand the elements for decades—or even centuries. Over time, these enduring objects take on a beautiful patina, as seen in this simple trough. (Turn to page 101 to learn how to age your galvanized planter.)

5 | **ELEGANT URNS:** One of the oldest container designs, urns have long been used across cultures for both ceremonial and practical purposes. Their graceful shapes and highly ornamented style lend a classical air to the garden.

1

2

4

3

5

# Advantages of Container Plantings

For beginners, busy gardeners, and those seeking vibrant accents for their home, containers are an easy and creative way to engage with the natural world. They're also an ideal solution for green thumbs in challenging climates or for plant enthusiasts who want to display a wide variety of specimens in a small space. Here are a few benefits of container plantings.

**PLANT A GARDEN ANYWHERE:** In urban settings, containers make it possible to grow plants on balconies and terraces, in window boxes, and even on vertical surfaces (see page 91). For those with more space, containers can be used to enhance patios, walkways, porches, and other outdoor living areas that can't support a permanent planting.

**ADD CONTRAST:** A well-placed container garden can soften and brighten a blank outdoor wall, a bare expanse of paved patio, or an entryway in need of framing. In these unadorned spaces, planters provide a welcome splash of organic color and texture.

**SPOTLIGHT EXCEPTIONAL SPECIMENS:** Containers can be used to set a singular plant apart from the surrounding landscape, drawing the viewer's eye to its noteworthy qualities. This is true of large-scale trees and shrubs—which become a garden focal point when paired with a statement planter—as well as smaller specimens with a notable scent or blooms that welcome closer examination.

**GROW A WIDER VARIETY OF PLANTS OUTSIDE:** In cooler climates, containers allow tender perennials—like palms and citrus trees—to be grown outside during the milder months, then moved indoors when the threat of frost arrives. Container plantings can also be used to showcase specimens that aren't suited to the soil type in your region.

**ROTATE AND CHANGE WITH THE SEASONS:** Containers offer the option to create short-term plantings that can be updated with relative ease, allowing for multiple, distinctive looks during one growing season. Individual plants can be highlighted during the peak of their beauty, then replaced as their blooms fade.

# Three Key Concepts for Container Garden Design

Renowned garden designer Gertrude Jekyll once advised: "The possession of a quantity of plants . . . does not make a garden; it only makes a collection. Having got the plants, the great thing is to use them with careful selection and definite intention." Three key elements—color, texture, and shape—should guide both the selection and the intention of a container garden. They offer a stable foundation for building a well-rounded planter, allowing the gardens of your imagination to thrive.

**1. COLOR:** Container plantings should adhere to a thoughtful, unified palette. There are many approaches to selecting the right colors for your planting. One is to choose plants in varying shades of a single color, creating a monochromatic effect—as with a collection of dark, moody foliage. Other color stories evolve through contrast and complement, with uniform greenery and tonal palettes enlivened by the blooms of brilliant specimens. (Find our favorite palettes beginning on page 55.)

**2. TEXTURE:** Diverse textures guide the eye through a planting. Texture extends beyond living matter—it also includes the container itself. In fact, three separate elements comprise the texture of a container garden: vessels, plants, and accents. The surface of the vessel should suit its contents; a sleek pot can support an array of textural plants, while rugged materials complement simpler specimens. The textures of the plants themselves should also be balanced; offset broad leaves with fine foliage, and add grasses or other elongated shapes where more interest is needed. If adding a topper such as gravel or wood chips for additional texture, choose this element last and keep the plants and vessel combination in mind. (For more on toppers, see page 52.)

**3. SHAPE:** Considerations of shape in container gardens are twofold: how do the shapes of the plants and vessel work together, and how does the shape of the container as a whole fit into its environment? For the first, keep in mind that a container's shape should highlight the most striking qualities of the plants inside. A hanging basket emphasizes the silhouette of spilling vines, while a graceful urn lends height to a pendulous plant. For the second, pinpoint the space that needs to be filled. Does the corner of an entryway lack vertical interest? Would an open expanse of patio benefit from a substantial centerpiece? As with color and texture, shape should also be balanced; busy surroundings benefit from a vessel with a simple silhouette, while the planter can take center stage in more subdued settings.

Texture is the star of this planting, which enlivens an unadorned corner of a patio with its lush silhouette. The spacious bowl makes room for complex textural layering of smooth allium leaves and spiky aloe with feathery foxtail ferns, trailing asparagus ferns, and wing fiber optic grass. Weathered wood chips at the base of the planting provide respite from the boisterous mix of foliage.

# Priming & Planting a Container Garden

While head-turning plants are a container garden's crowning glory, a thriving planter starts with strategically layered soil. Proper preparation assures that the plants in a container receive the necessary drainage, nutrients, and microbiology.

**STEP 1:** Make sure your vessel has a drainage hole. If it doesn't, drill one large enough for excess water to leave the soil. For planters that are too fragile or difficult to drill, fill the base with extra drainage medium (see step 2). Alternatively, leave plants in their grower's pots within the planter, so they can be lifted out to drain as needed.

**STEP 2:** Fill one-quarter of the planter with gravel or Growstone—a lightweight, stonelike medium made from recycled glass—to provide the drainage, aeration, and moisture control necessary for a healthy root system.

**STEP 3:** Add a layer of soil. (Peat-free soils are ideal, as they offer moisture retention and microbiology to help feed the plants over time.) For even more nutrition, mix the soil with nature's richest fertilizer: worm castings. Worm castings contain an active mixture of enzymes, bacteria, plant matter, manure remnants, and earthworm cocoons, resulting in a potent blend of water-soluble nutrients.

**STEP 4:** Dig a hole in the soil large enough for the root-ball of your plant and add a root-zone feeder pack, positioning it to touch the roots. Feeder packs offer concentrated fertilization along with biochar—a carbon-negative product that acts as a sponge for nutrients, microbiology, minerals, and water.

**STEP 5:** Place the plant on top of the feeder pack, then backfill the hole with additional potting soil, making sure the roots are completely covered.

**STEP 6:** If desired, top the soil with a layer of sheet moss to improve moisture retention.

**STEP 7:** Water thoroughly to activate microbes in the soil.

**STEP 8:** For optimal growth and blooming, apply a liquid fertilizer biweekly or monthly throughout the growing season.

# Topping It Off

The perfect combination of plant and vessel can be complemented by the judicious use of negative space. The addition of a natural topper such as gravel, slate, moss, or wood chips makes the most of the gap between a vertical specimen and its container, providing a clean field that allows the eye to rest and transition from focal plant to planter. Similarly, low-profile living specimens can be used as accents to fill out containers, a technique known as underplanting (see more about this on page 83). Toppers and underplantings help to soften any hard edges where planter and soil meet, and lend a finished appearance to your container garden.

1 | **RIVER STONES:** Use tumbled stones to add soft, natural texture to substantially sized plantings. River stones can also be mixed into a fine gravel topper as accents.

2 | **FRESH MOSS:** Sheet or clump moss makes for a lush, highly textured understory for small trees or plants with tall, slender stems.

3 | **CHARCOAL:** Use chunks of charcoal to create a high-contrast backdrop for plantings with graphic appeal, like a swirling collection of cacti.

4 | **SLATE SHARDS:** Lay pieces of slate flat atop the soil for a solid, smoky backdrop with a low profile, ideal for showcasing vines or creeping plants.

5 | **VERTICAL SLATE:** Carefully anchor shards of slate upright in the soil to form striking patterns, like this radial display surrounding a tall-stemmed specimen.

6 | **FINE GRAVEL:** Draw attention to plants with a unique silhouette or color by adding a layer of finely crushed gravel in a uniform, contrasting shade.

# 3

*Painterly Palettes*
## Seven Colorful Containers

As an artist animates a canvas by mixing the perfect pigments, a gardener brings
a container to life with colorful flowers and foliage. From pale, monochromatic
washes to the exuberant shades of spring, thoughtful palettes define a planting.
Cohesiveness and measured contrast in color leave room to take liberty with
other elements; a united palette allows for variation in texture, or the replacement
of flowering annuals for a seasonal refresh. The planters on the following pages
showcase the best and brightest color stories throughout the seasons, paired with
mix-and-match plant guides to customize each look at home.

## In This Planter:

1. Passionflower (*Passiflora* spp.)

2. *Dahlia* 'Karma Choc'

3. Fountain grass (*Pennisetum* 'Fireworks')

4. Sedge (*Carex* 'Silver Sceptre')

5. Blue grama grass (*Bouteloua gracilis* 'Blonde Ambition')

# Saturated Specimens

This overflowing display is informed by the Renaissance oil painting technique of chiaroscuro, in which a dramatic contrast between light and dark is used to emphasize three-dimensional forms.

**Options for Saturated Specimens:**

**DAHLIA** 'Karma Choc'

**COSMOS BIPINNATUS**

**ASTRANTIA MAJOR** 'Venice'

**AMARANTHUS CRUENTUS** 'Red Spike'

**ANGELICA GIGAS**

**AEONIUM ARBOREUM** 'Zwartkop'

**VIOLA × WITTROCKIANA** Frizzle Sizzle Burgundy

**LYSIMACHIA ATROPURPUREA** 'Beaujolais'

**SALVIA LYRATA** 'Purple Knockout'

### In This Planter:

1. Coleus
2. Black mondo grass (*Ophiopogon planiscapus* 'Nigrescens')

3. Black clover (*Trifolium repens* 'Atropurpureum')
4. *Petunia* 'Black Velvet' (aka 'Balpevac')

# Darkly Distinctive

This dramatic planting features a monochromatic collection of midnight blues and purples with black undertones. The moody foliage absorbs light, so this palette is best suited for a bright setting with minimal background clutter, where subtle variations in texture can be appreciated.

**Options for Darkly Distinctive:**

**PETUNIA** 'Black Velvet' (aka 'Balpevac')

**PHYSOCARPUS OPULIFOLIUS** All Black (aka 'Minall2')

**HELLEBORUS** 'Anna's Red'

**OXALIS VULCANICOLA** 'Zinfandel'

**FALSE INDIGO BUSH** (*Amorpha fruticosa*)

**BLACK MONDO GRASS** (*Ophiopogon planiscapus* 'Nigrescens')

### In This Planter:

1. *Dichondra argentea* 'Silver Falls'

2. Fiber optic grass (*Isolepis cernua*)

3. *Salvia apiana*

4. Bronze fennel (*Foeniculum vulgare* 'Purpureum')

# Color Washes

This subtle, sophisticated palette emphasizes the depth and variation within a single shade. The light sheen of the plants emphasizes textural contrast, while deeper colors at the center of the container make the highlights pop. The height of the graceful Willy Guhl Spindle shown opposite is further emphasized by the addition of "spillers" like the *Dichondra argentea* 'Silver Falls.'

**Options for Color Washes:**

**SEDUM LINEARE** 'Variegatum'

**PILEA DEPRESSA**

**PLECTRANTHUS ARGENTATUS**

**MUEHLENBECKIA COMPLEXA**

**SEDUM** spp.

**PILEA GLAUCA** 'Aquamarine'

## In This Planter:

1. *Carex* 'Everillo'

2. Arizona cypress (*Cupressus arizonica*)

3. *Rhus aromarica* 'Gro-Low'

# Shades of Green & Blue

Subtle color variation lets texture take center stage in this planted foliage trio. The contrasting silhouettes of sleek, draping fountain grass, frothy Arizona cypress, and leafy sumac are unified by an understated palette of greens and blues.

---

**Options for Shades of Green & Blue:**

**STINKING HELLEBORE**
(*Helleborus foetidus*)

**BLUE ARIZONA CYPRESS**
(*Cupressus arizonica* 'Blue Ice')

**ZINNIA ELEGANS** 'Green Envy'

**BLUE FESCUE** (*Festuca* 'Cool as Ice')

**OAKLEAF HYDRANGEA**
(*Hydrangea quercifolia* 'Little Honey')

**ECHEVERIA ELEGANS**

**SEDGE** (*Carex appalachica*)

**WHITE ONION ECHEVERIA**
(*Echeveria runyonii*)

**RHODODENDRON** spp.

## In This Planter:

1. Sweet alyssum (*Lobularia maritima*)

2. Black mondo grass (*Ophiopogon planiscapus* 'Nigrescens')

3. *Polystichum polyblepharum*

4. Lamb's ears (*Stachys byzantina*)

# Bright Whites

The play between light and shadow is key for this high-contrast color story. The freshness of the planted palette is echoed in the glaze of the vessel, lightened and textured by countless seasons in the garden.

**Options for Bright Whites:**

**ASTER**

**BACOPA** (*Sutera cordata*)

**COSMOS**

**CERASTIUM TOMENTOSUM**

**SAXIFRAGA × ARENDSII** Touran White (aka 'Rockwhite')

**DUSTY MILLER** (*Senecio cineraria*)

**VERBASCUM PHOENICEUM** 'Flush of White'

**CALOCEPHALUS** spp.

**TIARELLA** spp.

### In This Planter:

1. *Forsythia* × *intermedia*
2. Fountain grass (*Pennisetum setaceum* 'Fireworks')
3. *Heuchera* 'Delta Dawn'
4. Basket-of-gold alyssum (*Aurinia saxatilis* 'Compacta')
5. Eastern red columbine (*Aquilegia canadensis*)

# Tropical Spring

This riotous collection of blooms offers an explosion of sun-soaked hues to welcome spring. Anchored by golden forsythia, the vibrant flowers create a natural ombré effect in sherbet shades from lemon to grapefruit.

**Options for a Tropical Spring:**

**DAPPLED WILLOW** (*Salix integra* 'Hakuro-nishiki')

**DAHLIA** 'Bishop of Oxford'

**CAREX**

**PRIMULA OBCONICA** 'Salmon'

**ACER PSEUDOPLATANUS** 'Eskimo Sunset'

**DAHLIA** 'Karma Corona'

**GEUM** Totally Tangerine (aka 'Tim's Tangerine')

**BEGONIA** 'Peach Melba'

**SORBARIA SORBIFOLIA** 'Sem'

## In This Planter:

1. Lyme grass (*Leymus arenarius*)

2. Cardoon (*Cynara cardunculus*)

3. Tiger Eyes sumac (*Rhus typhina* 'Bailtiger')

4. Pineapple sage (*Salvia elegans*)

5. Culver's root (*Veronicastrum virginicum*)

6. *Hydrangea macrophylla*

7. *Cotoneaster* spp.

# Lemon & Lime

A celebration of color, this combination of citrus hues ranges from buttery yellow to citrine. Use this palette as a lively counterpoint to rugged planters, like a substantial fieldstone trough.

**Options for Lemon & Lime:**

**SPIDERWORT** (*Tradescantia* 'Sweet Kate')

**BIRD'S NEST FERN** (*Asplenium nidus*)

**GOLDENROD** (*Solidago* spp.)

**OXALIS VULCANICOLA** Molten Lava (aka 'Sunset Velvet')

**TIGER EYES SUMAC** (*Rhus typhina* 'Bailtiger')

**SEDUM MAKINOI** 'Ogon'

**CELOSIA ARGENTEA** var. **PLUMOSA** 'Century Yellow'

**FOUNTAIN GRASS** (*Miscanthus* spp.)

**GOLDEN ELDERBERRY** (*Sambucus nigra* subsp. *canadensis* 'Goldfinch')

# 4

*Design Ideas*

# Container Plantings Beyond the Basics

Container plantings are the perfect milieu for testing the waters of high garden style, easily scalable from a single pot to a towering green wall. In many cases, these uncommon plantings make an impact by introducing plants in unexpected places: by showcasing classic garden vegetables in a formal urn (page 73) or filling an unused fire pit with succulents (page 80). The natural beauties on the pages that follow will encourage your imagination—and your garden—to grow in new ways, and can be adapted to suit almost any space and level of expertise.

# Ornamental Vegetables & Herbs

A quintessential high-low look, the unexpected use of vegetables in decorative planters shines a spotlight on the beauty and diversity of edible plants. Ornamentals like kale, cabbage, and peppers are commonly found in fall containers, but the wider world of vegetables—especially the gorgeous variety of greens—offers a bounty of options for decorative planting.

LEFT: **AUTUMN MIX** Combine vegetables, herbs, and ornamentals for a planter that reflects the best of the entire garden—from flower bed to vegetable patch. In this autumn planting, the ruffled leaves of a colorful cabbage stand out against a backdrop of thyme and red thread alternathera.

OPPOSITE: **AN EDIBLE URN** A cluster of humble specimens including red-tinted sorrel (*Rumex sanguineus*), butter lettuce, and thyme contrasts with a formal urn edged in rusty scrollwork.

**STRIKING STRUCTURES** Pair a humble edible—like a simple cluster of butterhead lettuce, as above—with a stately urn to create an unexpected accent container in the vegetable patch. Rustic trellises and cloches are also excellent additions to vegetable plantings. Their woven construction and bold shapes offer architectural interest, and they can serve a practical purpose as support for vining varieties and protection from hungry critters.

# Hanging Baskets

There has long been something intriguing about the idea of plants cascading from the sky, famously evidenced by the mythical Hanging Gardens of Babylon, where flowers and foliage were said to pour down the terraces like waterfalls. Hanging baskets tap into this magic on a manageable scale, spilling plant life from above. These high-impact plantings connect garden to home, introducing greenery to porches and covered outdoor areas with limited space for cultivation. Turn to page 79 to learn how to plant a hanging basket.

---

## Trailing Plants

Draped over the edge of a suspended basket, long tendrils of greenery and flowers create striking silhouettes to enliven outdoor spaces.

**Chandelier plant (*Kalanchoe manginii*)**: Named for the shape created by its elegantly draped stems, this hardy succulent features vibrant, long-lasting flowers and prefers bright light and warm temperatures.

**Variegated ivy (*Hedera* spp.)**: The white markings of this rambling vine are caused by a lack of chlorophyll in areas of the leaf; this means that it's more sensitive to sunlight and will thrive in filtered sun or shade.

**House ivy (*Hedera* spp.)**: Native to Europe and western Asia, these shade-loving evergreen vines grow quickly for ample foliage.

**Verbena (*Verbena canadensis*)**: Blooming from late spring through first frost, verbena is a low-maintenance option for continuous color. Rich in nectar, its flowers will attract hummingbirds to hanging baskets.

**Jasmine (*Jasminum mesnyi*)**: Also known as primrose jasmine, this delicate climber is surprisingly hardy, needing little water to thrive.

---

**CASCADING VINES** A staggered group of hanging baskets puts the spotlight on dramatic spilling specimens for a large-scale display with vertical impact.

# Planting a Hanging Basket

With unusual forms and lofty locations, hanging baskets require a different approach to planting than a standard container.

TOP: **RENEWABLE MOSS LINER** Made from reclaimed fibers that have been tinted to achieve the look of natural moss, these liners are an environmentally friendly option with great water retention and drainage.

ABOVE: **WATER-SAVING FIBER LINER** Made from natural jute and coco fibers, these liners are biodegradable and pest resistant. They retain moisture well and promote air circulation for healthy root systems.

OPPOSITE: **SATURATED SUMMER** The bright blooms of dahlias, lantana, and crossandra provide vivid color in an unruly planting of many-hued foliage. When designing a hanging basket, achieve immediate color by packing in more plants than you would for a ground container; since baskets are a seasonal undertaking, there's no need to worry about plants outgrowing the space.

**STEP 1:** Select your basket and cut a liner from renewable moss or water-saving fiber to fit the bottom half of the basket (see photos at left). Creating a base for the planting, the liner secures the soil and retains moisture.

**STEP 2:** Soak the liner with water. If you'd like any plants to grow from the bottom of the basket, now is the time to place them: cut a few slits in the liner and insert trailing plants like sweet potato vine or lobelia that can grow downward.

**STEP 3:** Top off the basket with quality potting soil. Hanging basket soil should provide ample drainage and nutrition, since plants have limited space to root.

**STEP 4:** Fill the basket with a mix of healthy, well-established plants; check the root depth, as plants with very deep roots aren't suited for the limited space. Choose an imaginative mix of expansive, fast-growing species: clumpers, trailers, flowering plants, and foliage.

**STEP 5:** Select a sturdy hook (like a steel shepherd's hook) for hanging, as the basket's weight will increase once it's laden with soil and plants.

**STEP 6:** Water your basket more often than you would in-ground plantings, as the plants inside can't collect extra moisture from the environment. A long-reaching water wand makes it easier to access high areas.

**STEP 7:** Rotate the basket often to ensure that all sides receive even sunlight.

# Succulents in Bowls

Bowl planters are tailor-made homes for succulents, offering plentiful surface area to showcase the vibrancy and variety of these hardy specimens in multiplant groupings. Since they can be viewed from overhead, bowls filled with succulents also present a unique opportunity for patterned plantings; try concentric circles of tiny succulents surrounding a central specimen, or rows arranged by color for a gradient effect. Turn to page 205 for a few of our favorite jewel-tone succulents.

ABOVE: **A FIRE PIT PLANTING** When high-summer heat precludes their true purpose, fire pits find new life as succulent gardens. Their wide, shallow shape and built-in drainage are ideal for a large collection of succulents—like this graphic grouping in dusty greens and blues.

OPPOSITE: **A COLORFUL TRIO** Playful use of scale unites three hypertufa bowls, with distinctive palettes unified by statement-size specimens like black rose aeonium (*Aeonium arboreum* 'Zwartkop').

**A CARPET OF GREEN** Baby's tears (*Soleirolia soleirolii*) grow into open spaces
quickly and completely, making them an ideal choice for underplanting. Here,
they fill in an urn of Cape Primrose (*Streptocarpus* 'Black Panther') and ferns.

# Underplanted Containers

To create an underplanted container, choose focal plants like small trees, shrubs, and tall-stemmed perennials that leave open space on the surface of the soil, allowing small, low-growing specimens to be added as a secondary layer. Moss, trailing vines, and succulents all make excellent choices for underplantings, providing subtle interest in both color and texture to create dynamic designs. Especially tall focal specimens with slender trunks can also be paired with mid-height flowers or foliage for more dramatic layered styles (see page 35).

**STEP 1:** Select a focal plant that leaves sufficient space in the vessel for underplanting.

**STEP 2:** Choose your underplanting specimens, making sure that their moisture, temperature, and light needs are compatible with those of the focal plant.

**STEP 3:** Pot your focal plant as you normally would (see page 50), adding potting soil to the original soil line of the root-ball and packing as you build the base.

**STEP 4:** Dig a hole in the soil for each of the plants that will make up the underplanting. If you're adding a topper (gravel, slate, etc.) in addition to the smaller plants, cover their root-balls only halfway with soil so the topper can remain below their foliage and stems. Otherwise, fill in each hole as you normally would.

**STEP 5:** If adding a topper, scatter it onto the surface of the soil.

**STEP 6:** Once the plants are in the soil and any toppers are in place, water the container thoroughly. Be sure to consider the needs of all plants in the container when establishing an ongoing care routine. For example, underplanted specimens with shallow roots will need to be surface watered more frequently than the root-ball of a tree.

**HIGH CONTRAST** When choosing specimens for an underplanting, don't shy away from vibrant color combinations. In this hypertufa pot, an underplanting of chartreuse selaginella provides a field of vivid green that sets off the equally bright blooms of pink African violets.

# Plant Stands & Pot Feet

Planters can reach new heights with the addition of plant stands or pot feet. This supporting cast lends extra height when a final decorative touch is needed or to aid in ease of observation. They also serve a practical purpose during the winter months, preventing planters from freezing to the ground and sustaining damage over the winter months. At the tallest end of the spectrum, stately columns raise greens to eye level or beyond (see page 87). Low-profile options, like pot feet, provide subtle stylistic changes with protective benefits. For a natural look that will blend into the garden, select stands in materials that will weather over time, like steel with a rusted finish.

LEFT: **PRACTICAL POT FEET** An improvement to both style and function, boxy teak pot feet raise an unadorned taper planter just off the ground, allowing optimal drainage for a menagerie of tender succulents.

OPPOSITE: **AN ELEVATED COLLECTION** Angular teak pot feet provide modernist lines for paired planters with a midnight glaze, and echo the wooden legs of the third pot to create a cohesive grouping. The largest pot spotlights the dramatic foliage of *Alocasia*, while the smaller planters hold heuchera, euphorbia, and black mondo grass (*Ophiopogon planiscapus*).

# Planters in Rows

Tidy rows of perfectly matched planters bring structure to the garden, with creative applications that belie their conformist appearance. Height and definition are the key elements of this look, with simple shapes and clean lines providing cohesiveness to usher the eye through the collection with ease.

ABOVE: **IN GOOD ORDER** Rows of egg-shaped pots with a maritime glaze are topped with tidy hemispheres of boxwood to outline a pathway. Rusted by the seasons, metal stands elevate the planters for a bolder impact.

OPPOSITE: **GREAT HEIGHTS** Weighty columns take the place of traditional plant stands to create an eye-catching grouping that serves as an outdoor wall. Grassy bowls atop each column create the feeling of an overhead canopy.

# Garden Archways

Though most commonly seen as stately monuments, arches easily transform from Napoleonic to natural. These structures can provide an outdoor focal point, create a grand entrance, frame a view, or serve as a dividing element between two garden spaces. Their versatility in function is matched by their versatility in form; arches can be made from living hedges, foraged vines, weathered metal, or virtually any other sturdy material. No matter the medium, one factor unites these structures: their impact on the landscape.

OPPOSITE: **LIVING ARCHITECTURE** The formal, squared-off shape of a triumphal arch is softened by a planting of tiny foliage. The structure is a wooden frame mounted with window boxes, which are planted with *Tradescantia fluminensis*. Diligent pruning is needed for this look; for defined edges, regularly trim back any new growth that goes astray.

ABOVE: **TWINING VINES** Made from vining branches that have been trained into shape, this archway—ready for planting with flowering vines—acts as a threshold that leads from one area of the garden to another.

# Garden Wall Installations

Well worth the efforts of construction, planted installations offer room for growth in atypical and underutilized places, like along a backyard fence or the wall of a potting shed. The lofty ambitions of these installations are matched by their adaptability; from swaying grasses to winter greens, nearly any plant can thrive in a vertical garden with a bit of careful planning—and a tall ladder for planting season.

The biggest challenge in planting a green wall is creating an environment where plants can thrive high above the ground. An installation of hayracks with water-saving liners (shown opposite) offers an outstanding solution, with an ideal layout for adding concealed drip lines for irrigation. The depth of the rack also holds ample soil, where a mix of annuals, perennials, shrubs, and even small trees can take root. For long-lasting vertical installations, start with vessels made from heavy-gauge steel wire with a hot-dip galvanized finish; this practical combination will last for a hundred seasons in the garden.

**THE HEIGHT OF SUMMER** At the peak of growing season, nature perfects planted installations with untamed spills of foliage that blend and intertwine. After a few months of growth, waterfalls of *Ipomea*, *Solidago*, castor bean plant (*Ricinus communis*), and *Hibiscus* 'Mahogany Splendor' fully obscured this wall of hayrack planters.

LEFT: **A VINE CANOPY** This towering wall measures 32 feet high. The striking foliage of oakleaf hydrangea stands out against the amaranthus, grasses, and sedum, providing crucial variance in this gigantic garden.

OPPOSITE: **GREEN GEOMETRY** Antique funnels take the place of traditional planters against this well-weathered wall. Arranged in a grid, the funnels offer a top-down watering solution; water poured into the highest funnels is routed into those below.

# 5

*Seasonal Stars*

# A Year of Planters

In his 1664 almanac, *Kalendarium Hortense*, the celebrated English diarist and horticulturist John Evelyn wrote, "The gardener's work is never at an end; it begins with the year, and continues into the next; he prepares the ground, and then he sows it; after that he plants, and then he gathers the fruits." Evelyn's sentiments still hold true today—every page on the calendar brings new appeal to the garden. Spring's first flush of eager flowers and tender greens gives way to the overflowing bounty of summer, with the burnished hues and golden light of autumn just behind. Even winter has its charms, with fresh-fallen snow providing a dazzling backdrop for bright berries, evergreen boughs, and red dogwood stems. Container gardens offer up the best of each season's landscape in miniature, with high-impact statements spotlighting the year's most beloved—and eagerly awaited—flowers and foliage.

# A Layered Spring Bulb Garden

As the most anticipated time of year for gardeners, it always seems that spring can't come quickly enough. When the weather still feels like winter, container plantings can usher in the new season early. Often the first faces to appear in our gardens, bulbs provide a welcome burst of color to kick off spring.

A flourishing bulb planter requires some forethought; many bulbs must be planted in the season opposite to their bloom time. Popular spring bloomers—like irises, tulips, and hyacinths—should be placed in the soil in autumn, where they'll await the first warm days of the following year to come alive. If planted in fall, these spring-blooming bulbs should be overwintered under cover in a dark, cool (35°F to 45°F) location—a garage is often ideal. If you're planting at winter's end, seek out nurseries that offer bulbs that were chilled for several weeks to simulate cold weather, which allows them to be planted later for spring flowers. In either case, a bulb container garden should be layered based on bloom times, with late bloomers planted at the deepest point and early-blooming bulbs above.

The preceding principles were used to create the container featured on the following pages, planted in advance with layers of bulbs that will bloom from March through May. This single planter provides continuous color in three distinctive looks, with wild branches giving way to ruffled tulips and giant alliums as the season progresses.

**THE WINTER WAIT** When the first flowers are still a few weeks away, the planter derives muted color from a topper of moss and cut heather, accented with seeded eucalyptus, hazelnut stems, fantail pussy willow, curly willow, and rosemary. Once the bulbs begin to grow, pull away the heather and a few branches to make room for the stems, letting some branches remain as a supportive armature for the sprouting foliage.

**EARLY SPRING** First to emerge, a bright crop of Minnow and Pink Mix daffodils and grape hyacinths (*Muscari*) fills the planter in March. Winter's moss topper remains, along with curly willow branches for support. The willow stems may sprout a few leaves of their own, making the perfect accent for cheery daffodils and tiny hyacinths.

**MAY FLOWERS** The ever-evolving garden blooms once more in late spring. Bold and bright, ruffled 'Princess Irene' tulips pair with spiky 'Gladiator' giant allium against a backdrop of vibrant greens. The curly willow stems linger in the planter to brace these tall flowers, which will enliven outdoor spaces as the rest of the garden awakens.

# Carefree Summer Greens

When the long, sunny days of midsummer arrive, let your pruners and watering cans take a well-earned vacation with low-maintenance plantings. Thoughtfully planted containers can withstand a bit of neglect during weekend getaways and intense heat waves. Curate collections of plants that look best when they're gnarly and natural for overgrown containers that reflect the season's abundance—no garden snips required. And seek out specimens that thrive in hot, dry conditions for plantings that won't wilt if you miss a few days of watering.

**GROWING WILD** *Overgrowth* is the word of the moment when summer reaches its peak. Plants cultivated without intensive pruning bring an organic feel to container gardens. Spilling through the framework of a wall-mounted basket, a hardy planting of sedum, yellow yarrow, lavender, and fountain grass reveals wild and wonderful character with minimal upkeep.

**BEAT THE HEAT** Let a single, drought-tolerant specimen—like this heat-loving olive tree— take the spotlight for an impactful planting that can withstand summer extremes. Set off the foliage with a planter in a contrasting shade; here, a galvanized metal barrel nods to the season in sun-bleached silver.

## HOW TO AGE A GALVANIZED PLANTER

Give brand-new galvanized objects a century of weathering in just one week.

1. Pretreat and clean the surface of the zinc to remove any existing grease and oxidation. Wipe down the exterior with a 5 percent solution of sulfuric acid, then rinse thoroughly.

2. Treat the object with a solution of 200 grams of iron chloride added to 1 liter of water, or 1 teaspoon copper sulfate and 2 teaspoons table salt added to 1 liter of water.

3. Leave in a sunny location for one week, spraying regularly with salt water, until the desired aging is achieved.

# Heirloom Pumpkin Towers

Pumpkins are the undisputed stars of the fall garden, and their decorative potential extends far beyond the traditional jack-o'-lantern. As the growing season ends for climbing and vining plants, repurpose garden structures as the framework for tall stacks of heirloom pumpkins. With countless cultivars from tiny 'Baby Boo' to giant 'Prizewinner' and colors ranging from deep orange to pale blue, pumpkins offer lots of options for decorative use. (Find a guide to our favorite heirloom varieties on page 267.) Towering displays of pumpkins offer a fresh way to showcase these autumn A-listers, no carving tools required.

ABOVE: **SHADES OF AUTUMN** As climbing vines begin to fade, refresh planter-and-trellis pairings with stacks of heirloom pumpkins that echo the colors of fall foliage.

TOP: **AN EARLY-FALL ENTRYWAY** Use tall stacks of a single pumpkin variety as a high-impact frame for the doorway. Here, heirloom specimens with mottled skin mirror the lingering green foliage of early autumn.

OPPOSITE: **OMBRÉ ORANGE** Showcase autumn's warm hues by creating an ombré collection of pumpkins inside a tapered garden tuteur. To achieve the perfect stack, select pumpkins with flattened shapes in graduated sizes.

# Snowbound Specimens

Winter can feel like a time of stasis in the garden, with planters stowed away and perennials deep under the snow, awaiting spring's invitation to return. However, life can still be found in abundance. Bright branches and resilient evergreens pop against an all-white backdrop, while uniquely shaped plants become sculptures after snowfall. These reminders of nature's bounty carry us through the coldest months, and brighten celebrations at year's end.

**SHAPES IN THE SNOW** Arrange branches with striking silhouettes in anticipation of snowfall; once coated in snow, this urn of knotty magnolia twigs serves as an outdoor art piece.

ABOVE: **BRILLIANT BRANCHES**
Snow-dusted eucalyptus
offers lacy texture, and
will hold its shape without
disintegrating during the
winter months. Orange
winterberries peek out from
among the stems for an
unexpected flash of color.

LEFT: **NATURAL ORNAMENTS**
Foraged Osage oranges, the
inedible fruit of *Maclura
pomifera*, serve as vibrant
accent pieces in winter
plantings thanks to their
chartreuse rind and knobby
texture.

# Spotlight on Summer

*bloom & beauty*

———

The garden greets summer's arrival with a jubilee. Every plant unfurls its celebratory banners in the form of lush leaves, brilliant blooms, and climbing vines. The table groans under the weight of the high-season harvest, filled with heirloom tomatoes, juicy melons, piquant peppers, and crisp greens. Flowers vie for attention in overflowing beds, their radiant faces turning upward to bask in the sun. Birds sing, honeybees buzz, and cicadas hum through the nights in a joyful chorus.

In this most bountiful of seasons, the natural world invites us to join it in celebration. We're beckoned outside by its sun-drenched afternoons, green expanses of lawn and field, and mild, golden-lit evenings. It is a season to create, to cultivate, and to embrace the abundance of the landscape around us.

# High-Summer Fields at Laughing Lady Flower Farm

At the peak of summer, in a quiet neighborhood in Doylestown, Pennsylvania, Laughing Lady Flower Farm comes alive with colorful blooms. Founder Kate Sparks heads to the fields bright and early, taking stock of her stems and planning beautiful bouquets in the hazy morning light.

Kate and her family came to Doylestown in 1989, after spending ten years abroad in Switzerland. She started growing herbs for the catering business she owned at the time, and eventually branched out to a few types of flowers. Her passion for flower farming soon blossomed, and the family moved to the four-acre plot that would become Laughing Lady; she has been growing there since 1998. A self-taught farmer and floral designer, she now offers her blooms at markets across the region and designs entire weddings using flowers from her own farm, even walking brides through the fields to select their stems.

The wild and wonderful array of flowers found in Kate's compact fields is reflected in her naturalistic design philosophy. She loves lush, fresh arrangements with lots of movement, showcasing the natural colors, textures, and scents of seasonal flowers. Most of her arrangements find their way to recycled vases, collected during her trips to antiques and vintage shops.

Though summer brings a lull between the hectic wedding seasons of spring and autumn, the fields at Laughing Lady are busy blooming. July brings a bounty of outstanding flowers, including giant 'Incrediball' hydrangeas, towering joe-pye weed, vibrant foxgloves, and chocolate laceflower. The first dahlias also emerge, taking their place alongside cosmos, yarrow, nigella, rudbeckia, silver dollar eucalyptus, and countless other stems for dazzling summer bouquets.

# Summer Nights

As summer comes to Scandinavia, daylight hours extend to remarkable lengths—the solstice in Stockholm offers an astonishing eighteen and a half hours of sunlight! All that sun is cause for celebration, since December days in the region see just six hours of light. To take advantage of these long and pleasant days, citizens in Nordic countries observe a number of traditions on Midsummer Eve, celebrated at the end of June to mark the solstice.

**MAYPOLES:** Many Swedes begin their summer holidays on Midsummer Eve and head to the countryside. Family and friends spend the day gathering flowers and foliage, which are used to decorate the maypole, more accurately known as a *midsommarstång* or "midsummer pole." Once the maypole is raised, it serves as the centerpiece for an evening of traditional dancing and singing.

**BONFIRES:** In Norway and Denmark, the maypole is replaced by a roaring bonfire at Midsummer Eve celebrations.

Especially popular in coastal regions, towering community bonfires are usually accompanied by singing, dancing, and plentiful grilled food.

**HERRING & POTATOES:** At Swedish celebrations, a Midsummer Eve menu isn't complete without pickled herring and boiled new potatoes, garnished with sour cream, chives, and fresh dill. The season's first strawberries—topped with cream—also appear at traditional feasts.

**SEVEN FLOWERS:** In Scandinavian folklore, Midsummer Eve is considered a magical time for love. It's said that a young woman should pick seven different flowers on the night of the celebration; tucked beneath her pillow, the flowers will inspire dreams of the man she'll marry.

# Wreaths All Around

---

## 1

### GATHER FROM THE GARDEN
*Our Wreath Philosophy* 123

## 2

### WREATHS
*Materials & Making* 129

## 3

### FULL CIRCLES
*Seven Wreath Projects* 141

## 4

### DESIGN IDEAS
*Wreaths Beyond the Basics* 157

In ancient Greece and Rome, a humble wreath of laurel leaves served as the symbol for society's highest honors. Simple laurel circlets were presented to renowned poets, victorious commanders in battle, and—most famously—Olympic champions. From this practice, we derive the modern term "poet laureate," the title conferred on a nation's most esteemed scribe. Wreaths have since become important symbols of both sorrow and celebration, laid in memoriam or hung with joy to mark holidays throughout the year.

As their symbolic meanings have expanded, so too have their materials; lush collections of fresh, dried, faux, and even metal botanicals offer everlasting color for designs that celebrate the best of each season. Today, wreaths are most commonly seen at the doorstep, but we find them equally suited for display throughout the home. The following pages feature wreaths for every season, from green spring circlets to mossy winter rings. (Holiday wreaths and greens can be found in A Natural Holiday, beginning on page 284.) Their variations are as endless as their circular form, ranging from simple garden greetings at the entryway to grand installations for outdoor spaces.

PREVIOUS PAGES: The colors and textures of the autumn forest are celebrated in this long-lasting wreath, made from layers of dried, preserved, and faux finds including maple leaves and seed pods, preserved and dyed shelf mushrooms, reindeer moss, and metal botanicals.

RIGHT: A gallery-style installation showcases the diversity of wreaths in both materials and style, pairing dense collections of dried and preserved blooms with slender circlets of fresh vine. For more on wreath groupings, see page 160.

# 1

*Gather from the Garden*

## Our Wreath Philosophy

The term "wreath" is derived from the Old English *writha*, meaning a band or twist. This etymological origin highlights the defining quality of a wreath: its circular form, symbolic of the cycle of the seasons and the endless renewal of the natural world. Beyond shape, very few rules govern the making and use of a wreath. The design may be orderly and formal or wild and impromptu. The materials may be preserved for lasting impact or freshly foraged for fleeting, seasonal beauty. Finally, the presentation may be as simple as an individual circlet in the window or as complex as a layered and illuminated chandelier. The guiding concepts that follow can be adapted to suit designs of any scale, space, and season.

# Forage for Seasonal Materials

The quintessential seasonal accent, wreaths celebrate what we see in nature, and invite those materials into the home. To capture an of-the-moment spirit in your designs, head outdoors to collect finds from the garden or forest. Gather large bundles of branches and twigs to make a wreath from scratch, or tiny, individual flowers to accent an existing circlet of metal or faux botanicals. When designing a wreath, embrace the imperfections of found and foraged elements. A shaggy branch, curling leaf, or gracefully fading bloom brings home the ever-changing beauty of the natural world. (Find a guide to wreath-making materials on pages 131–135.)

ABOVE: Foraging trips during the colder months can offer unexpected accents—like lichen-covered branches, curling bark, moss, and pinecones—that add texture to a simple twig wreath.

OPPOSITE: The canny forager can collect stems from nearby gardens and meadows to dry or preserve, extending the enjoyment of nature's bounty through the year. (See page 135 for a guide to preserving botanicals.)

# Incorporate High & Low Elements

A thoughtful mix of everyday and elevated ingredients helps to reimagine the familiar styles and functions of wreaths. For an unexpected look that mingles high and low materials, pair delicate blooms with rugged branches, or use a length of colorful silk ribbon to suspend a sparse circlet of twigs. Where and how a wreath is displayed can also yield surprising high-low juxtapositions. Adorn the garden shed with an elegant ring of lush blooms, or allow a wild wreath of foraged finds to spill over the sharp angles of a classically appointed mantel.

OPPOSITE: A wild tangle of vine slung casually over a weathered fence post gains an elevated touch from a layer of finely detailed zinc leaves. This durable combination will last through many seasons, gradually transforming into a garden antique.

ABOVE: An organically shaped wreath of bare twigs remakes an existing light fixture for autumn, serving as a rustic and unexpected take on the sophisticated chandelier.

# 2

*Wreaths*

# Materials & Making

Hung at the center of the door, in a sunny window, or above the mantel, a wreath serves as a vibrant greeting that welcomes friends, visitors, and passers-by. Wherever they're displayed, wreaths also set the tone for seasonal décor, introducing colors and materials that reflect the world outside. The following pages survey our favorite wreath-making components, followed by practical, step-by-step techniques for transforming these materials into striking seasonal displays.

# Wreath-Making Components

Materials are the most important feature of any wreath, dictating both its location and longevity. A fresh wreath makes a short-lived seasonal accent that will thrive in outdoor spaces, while preserved botanicals are perfectly suited to indoor display. Wreath components can be broadly divided into four categories—fresh, dried, faux, and preserved—each with its own merits and applications.

## *Fresh Foliage*

Though ephemeral, fresh wreaths showcase the best stems of a season. When making a fresh wreath, consider botanicals that have a long vase life, or those that dry gracefully for extended display. Good options include spring-budding or -flowering branches; mosses; summer vines like bittersweet and sturdy flowers like yarrow, strawflower, and grass plumes; fall foliage branches, nuts, and gourds; and winter greens, pods, and seed heads. Fresh wreaths are ideal for outdoor use, particularly during the colder months; they benefit from natural rainfall, and will last longer when not exposed to artificial heating.

ABOVE: Festooned with glossy leaves, simple circlets of fresh vines make a summer statement.

LEFT: The abundant buds and catkins of early spring add texture to unruly wreaths of bare branches.

## Dried Stems

Perhaps the most familiar wreath-making materials, dried flowers and foliage offer the look of fresh stems with months—or even years—of added longevity. These materials extend the beauty of the garden, preserving what was most attractive in the spring and summer landscape for enjoyment year-round. Delicate dried stems are best suited to indoor or sheltered outdoor display; their fragile petals and leaves can't withstand the wind and moisture of exposed outdoor locations.

When made with dried elements, wreaths can showcase a mix of blooms and foliage from any season and habitat, providing limitless options for color and texture combinations. Try mixing botanicals from multiple seasons in a single wreath, or hanging two wreaths that reflect different seasons side by side. Here, sheaves of autumn wheat (above) make surprising companions for summer's berry-hued blooms and vibrant greens (below).

## *Faux & Metal*

For an everlasting accent indoors and out, consider a wreath made of faux stems or metal botanicals. Mimicking the look of natural components, these enduring materials can make permanent displays on their own or serve as the base for a rotating cast of more delicate fresh and dried stems.

Metal and faux foliage mingle on this layered wreath, which pairs soft faux cedar with iron allium blooms. This sturdy combination is well suited for outdoor locations, as it's able to withstand the elements through a long autumn and winter.

## *Preserved Botanicals*

A step beyond dried stems, preserved flowers and foliage offer exceptionally lifelike color and flexibility for wreaths. The preserving process replaces the water content of a fresh stem with a glycerin solution; this maintains the original color and texture more effectively than drying, which can cause some leaves and petals to fade and become brittle. Preserved wreaths do require a bit of additional care: avoid placing glycerin-preserved specimens in intense sunlight, heat, or humidity, which will shorten their life span and potentially cause glycerin drips.

## HOW TO PRESERVE LEAVES AND FERNS WITH GLYCERIN

A dip into a simple solution of glycerin and water creates preserved botanicals with a perpetually supple, fresh appearance. Glycerin preservation results in stems with significant flexibility, making them adaptable to wreaths of any shape and style.

**What You'll Need:**
- Fresh leaves and fern fronds
- Garden snips
- Glycerin
- Shallow container, large enough to submerge stems
- Large platter
- Paper towels
- Book or sheet of glass (for pressing)

1. Gather the botanicals you'd like to preserve—the fresher the better.

2. Use garden snips to recut the stems at an angle while holding them underwater; this creates extra surface area for absorption and removes any air bubbles, which can block the uptake of the glycerin solution.

3. Mix the glycerin solution. Combine one part glycerin and two parts warm water (approximately 135°F) in a vessel large enough to hold all the leaves when laid flat.

4. One at a time, fully submerge the leaves in the solution.

5. Once all the leaves are in place, position a flat platter or tray over the container and weight it down so all leaves remain completely submerged. Let soak for two to three days.

6. Extract the leaves from the solution. If they have clumped, carefully separate and rinse them under warm water to remove any excess glycerin.

7. Gently unfold and reshape the leaves as needed, and place them on a paper towel to dry. Cover them with a book or sheet of glass so they remain flat.

8. Once fully dry, the lifelike leaves can be incorporated into wreaths, garlands, and arrangements.

Glycerin-preserved stems make a lush addition to mixed botanical wreaths, but they truly shine as stand-alone statements, like these circlets formed from single fern fronds. These graceful wreaths require fronds with significant flexibility, which makes glycerin preservation preferable to traditional drying methods.

# Wreath-Making Basics

The wreath-making process allows for a great deal of creative freedom when it comes to shape, style, and seasonality. The instructions below can be adapted to make a variety of wreaths, using either a wreath form or shaped twigs, paired with your choice of materials (see pages 131-135).

## *Making a Wreath Using a Form*

Use a foam or straw base to structure an abundant moss-covered wreath to suit all seasons.

### What You'll Need:
- Fresh, preserved, or faux botanical accents
- Foam or straw wreath base (available at craft and floral supply stores)
- Fresh or preserved reindeer and clump moss
- Glue gun or floral picks (available at craft and floral supply stores)
- Garden snips

**STEP 1:** Gather your materials. Choose fresh elements for a temporary wreath, or preserved and faux materials for a more permanent look.

**STEP 2:** Cover the base in an even layer of reindeer moss, securing with hot glue or floral picks (the latter is preferable for fresh moss). Then add pieces of clump moss and different colors of reindeer moss, if desired.

**STEP 3:** Use garden snips to trim the botanical elements to scale, so each piece fits comfortably on the base.

**STEP 4:** Layer in smaller botanicals, such as small succulents and fresh evergreen sprigs (pictured here), and secure with hot glue or floral picks. (Hot glue will preserve succulents' roots for a few weeks with daily misting.)

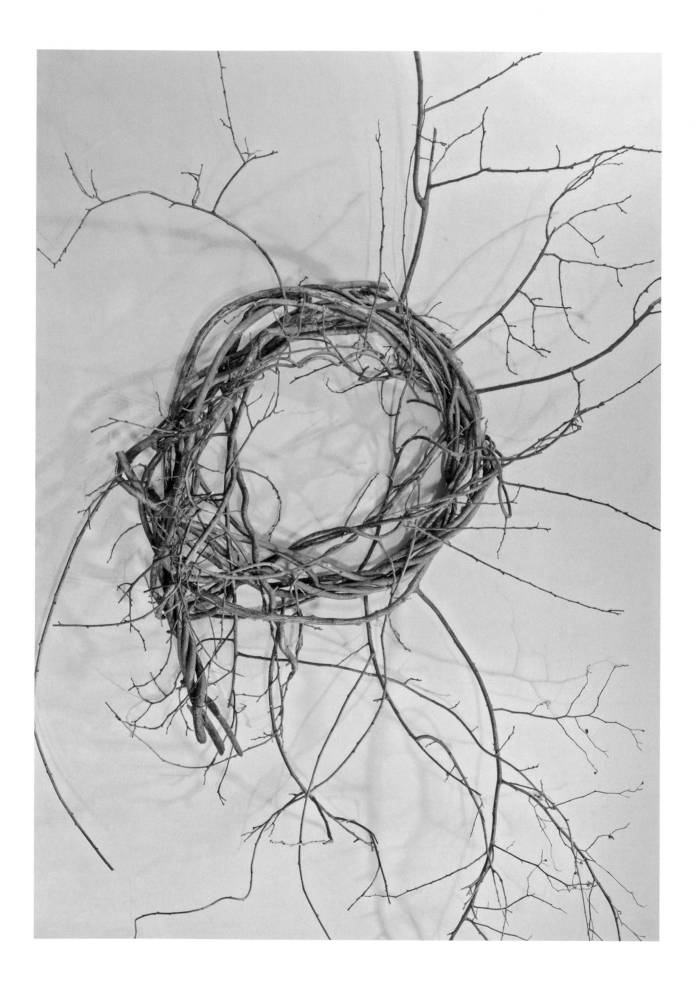

# Making a Free-Form Branch Wreath

Some wreaths, like the one shown opposite, don't rely on a form for structure. Instead, they're simply made from fresh, flexible branches. Try this method for a wild and wonderful look with an eye-catching asymmetrical silhouette.

**What You'll Need:**
- Flexible twigs
- Garden snips
- Floral wire
- Wire snips
- Moss, tillandsia, or succulents (optional)
- Glue gun (optional)

**STEP 1:** Gather your twigs. Curly willow, pussy willow, and dogwood are options with good flexibility, which is key for this method. Be sure the twigs don't snap when bent.

**STEP 2:** Determine the size of your wreath by bending one twig into a circular form. Using garden snips, trim the twig until the ends can meet in a circle of your desired diameter.

**STEP 3:** Use the first twig as a guide to trim several more twigs to the same length.

**STEP 4:** Bend the trimmed twigs into a circle to form the base of the wreath, joining the ends with floral wire to create the circle.

**STEP 5:** Once the base is formed, use floral wire to attach additional branches or other botanicals as desired. Leave the ends of some branches loose for a wild, asymmetrical shape.

**STEP 6:** Use wire snips to trim away any excess wire.

**STEP 7:** If desired, layer the wreath with moss, tillandsia, succulents, or other natural embellishments. Secure the embellishments with floral wire or a dot of hot glue, or simply tuck them among the twigs.

# 3

*Full Circles*

## Seven Wreath Projects

A wreath takes shape in many layers, from the sturdiest boughs to the smallest berries. These botanical works of art can be meditative in the making, whether weaving a base of branches and vines or foraging for flowers and foliage. The projects in the following pages can be followed to the letter for a picture-perfect wreath, or adapted to accommodate seasonal materials and your personal style.

# A Centerpiece Constellation

A dramatic alternative to the traditional centerpiece, this look begins with a trio of metal rings as a foundation. The rings provide structure for a layered mix of wild vines, fresh foliage, faux stems, and sparkling light strands that forms a starry sky above the table. For an alternative light look, swap the strand of lights for tapers at the center of each sphere (see page 140).

## What You'll Need:
- 3 iron rings in graduated sizes, with hanging chains
- Dried grapevine
- Floral wire
- Wire snips
- Fresh amaranth blooms
- Fresh chinaberry (*Melia azedarach*)
- Fresh kangaroo paw branches (*Anigozanthos flavidus*)
- Fresh pepperberry (*Schinus molle*)
- Dried sea oats (*Uniola paniculata*)
- Faux sumac
- Faux berries
- Battery-powered lights (several thin, wire strands with small LED bulbs work best)

**STEP 1:** Separate pieces of the grapevine and tie them loosely around each circle, attaching them to the ring with floral wire.

**STEP 2:** Working from the center of the largest ring to establish a focal point, affix a mixture of the fresh, dried, and faux foliage on the lower third of each wreath with floral wire, letting the amaranth, sumac, and kangaroo paw branches trail downward.

**STEP 3:** Weave the lights around each wreath, overlapping the strands several times and letting the ends hang downward to highlight the trailing stems.

# Natural Asymmetry

For a contemporary approach to wreath making, consider an asymmetrical silhouette. A durable collection of faux botanicals, dried heather, and weathered metal leaves makes this wreath a year-round favorite. Clustered faux succulents form the focal point of the design, paired with aged metal fern fronds for a tropical touch that can endure through even the coldest winters.

**What You'll Need:**
- Metal laurel leaves and fern fronds (ours came from ShopTerrain.com)
- Grapevine wreath base (see page 139 to learn how to make your own)
- Floral wire
- Wire snips
- Dried heather
- Faux scabiosa
- Faux succulents
- Faux sedum

**STEP 1:** Begin by placing the metal laurel leaves and fern fronds near the bottom right of the wreath base, pointing in opposite directions with the bases of the leaves and fronds nearly touching.

**STEP 2:** Gently bend the metal stems to match the curve of the wreath base, then fasten them to the grapevine with floral wire.

**STEP 3:** Layer stems of dried heather onto the wreath and attach with floral wire, beginning at the point where the metal stems meet and working around the circle.

**STEP 4:** Add clusters of faux scabiosa, layered on top of the metal stems and attached with wire.

**STEP 5:** Arrange three large faux succulents in a corsage at the point where the metal stems meet, then add trailing faux sedum below and around the succulents.

**STEP 6:** Attach the succulents and sedum with wire to complete the wreath.

# Metal in the Mix

A circle of iron oak leaves serves as the structure for this vibrantly colored wreath, supporting tiny bundles of fresh foliage and faux fruit in the rich hues of harvest season. This bundling technique means that the metal frame can be reimagined again and again; it's simple to swap out the small bunches whenever fresh stems become available in the garden.

## What You'll Need:

- Fresh purple beech leaves (*Fagus sylvatica* f. *purpurea*)
- Fresh fountain grass (*Pennisetum*)
- Fresh shortleaf pine sprigs (*Pinus echinata*)
- Faux crab apple branches
- Faux raspberry branches
- Faux berry branches (winterberry, bittersweet, or similar)
- Garden snips
- Floral wire
- Wire snips
- Metal botanical wreath (ours came from ShopTerrain.com)

**STEP 1:** Gather a variety of fresh and faux botanicals. (If you'd like to display the wreath permanently without updating the botanicals, use all faux.)

**STEP 2:** Once your stems are gathered, snip small pieces that match the scale of the metal botanicals.

**STEP 3:** Sort the snipped stems into tiny bundles of mixed cuttings. Be sure to include one or two stems of each botanical in each bundle.

**STEP 4:** Use floral wire to secure each bundle, wrapping snugly around the stems near the base.

**STEP 5:** Anchor the bundles to the frame of the wreath with loops of floral wire, tucking the fresh cuts between the metal leaves. Space the bundles evenly along the frame for a lush, balanced appearance.

**STEP 6:** When the fresh cuts begin to fade or wilt, repeat steps 1 through 5 to rejuvenate your wreath.

# A Forager's Mantelpiece

An overscaled focal point for a classically styled living room, this wreath is made from a mix of foraged vines and dyed botanicals, balancing the muted shades of dried and preserved materials with brighter stems for whimsical color. An organic base of bittersweet vine gives the wreath lots of movement, as do the fluttering, silvery leaves of dried silverberry (*Elaeagnus*). The lush textures and exaggerated asymmetry of the design are well suited to a minimalist backdrop, like this crisp combination of cool gray marble and white trim.

## What You'll Need:

- Bittersweet vine
- Tarp
- Matte spray sealant
- Floral wire
- Wire snips
- Dried silverberry branches
- Preserved fan palm
- Dried eucalyptus (dyed, deep orange or red, if available)
- Fresh winterberry
- Dried thistle
- Dried kangaroo paw
- Metal fern garland (ours came from ShopTerrain.com)

**STEP 1:** Start by gathering long, wispy pieces of bittersweet vine (up to several feet in length, depending on the desired scale of your wreath).

**STEP 2:** Place the vine on a tarp outdoors and spray with a matte sealant to protect against berry dispersal; let dry. Be sure to prevent any berries from dropping outdoors (see note on page 150).

**STEP 3:** To keep the base airy, weave the vine loosely into a rough circle, allowing it to retain its natural movement. Secure the ends of the circle with floral wire if needed.

**STEP 4:** Create a large "brooch" with the remaining botanicals, starting with large silverberry branches as the base and densely layering the fan palm, eucalyptus, winterberry, thistle, and kangaroo paw. Fasten the brooch to the lower corner of the wreath using floral wire.

**STEP 5:** Scatter a few additional cuttings of silverberry and winterberry around the perimeter of the wreath for a wilder silhouette.

**STEP 6:** Twine the fern garland through the negative space opposite the brooch, allowing it to weave naturally and spill off the bottom of the circle in an effortless gesture to complete the look.

# Fall Berries & Foliage

This loosely layered wreath requires just two components: foraged vines and a flexible garland. It begins with a base of bittersweet, which looks its brightest in late fall or early winter—making it a perfect accent piece for the harvest doorstep. This recipe can be adapted for any season by gathering fresh vines—from summer honeysuckle to winter ivy—and structuring them with the help of a flexible garland.

## What You'll Need:

- Fresh bittersweet vine
- Garden snips
- Tarp
- Matte spray sealant
- Floral wire
- Wire snips
- Metal garland (ours came from ShopTerrain.com)

**A NOTE ON BITTERSWEET** American bittersweet is easily confused with highly invasive Oriental bittersweet, which produces damaging vines that can overtake the landscape. Oriental bittersweet should be removed whenever it's found; if you'd like to use the uprooted vines in seasonal décor, be sure to treat them with a matte spray sealant so the berries can't spread.

A couple of key features can help in identification. American bittersweet has berries only at the end of its stem, while the berries of Oriental bittersweet are scattered along the length of the vine. American bittersweet features orange seed capsules on red berries, while Oriental bittersweet has yellow seed capsules on red berries.

**STEP 1:** Start by gathering fresh bittersweet vine in late autumn, when its bright berries emerge. Cut a single length of vine for a small, simple circlet, or several pieces for a larger wreath with multiple layers.

**STEP 2:** Place the vine on a tarp outdoors and spray with a matte sealant to prevent berry dispersal; let dry. Be sure no berries drop outdoors.

**STEP 3:** Once the vine is sealed, shape it into a loose circle, wrapping it a few times for a fuller shape if desired. It's best to shape the wreath right away, while the vine is still flexible.

**STEP 4:** Connect the ends with floral wire as needed, then wrap the metal garland around the vine base. The garland will help the vine retain its shape for display.

# A Glowing Garden Chandelier

A clever three-pronged hanger is at the heart of this wreath, placed horizontally above an outdoor table to create an unconventional chandelier. Reindeer moss serves as the base for this summer style, but any monoculture wreath can be used as a foundation; try eucalyptus for spring or fresh evergreen boughs for a winter variation. Hang a pair of these wreath displays from a patio pergola to create an inviting outdoor dining space.

## What You'll Need:
- Premade reindeer moss wreath
- Metal wreath hanger
- Metal flower garland (ours came from ShopTerrain.com)
- Wire LED light strands
- Fresh vines
- Floral wire (optional)
- Wire snips (optional)

**STEP 1**: Place the wreath in the hanger and begin wrapping it with the metal garland.

**STEP 2**: Leave one end of the garland loose, and wrap it upward onto an arm of the hanger.

**STEP 3**: Starting from the top, twine the light strands around the arms of the hanger, letting the ends dangle through the center of the wreath.

**STEP 4**: Arrange the fresh vines loosely around the wreath, allowing some ends to reach outward for a natural silhouette. (Use floral wire to anchor pieces of the vine, if needed.)

# A Woodland Ring

A statement piece for a large outdoor wall, this oversize wreath is a permanent installation. Its clean, subtly geometric shape is made up of individual segments of birch logs. The steps below can be followed to make a double-ring wreath that's 6 feet in diameter, with ten sides made from individual log segments. As the holidays approach, try adding layers of lights and greens to the birch base for added cheer. (See more festive wreath ideas in A Natural Holiday, beginning on page 284.)

## What You'll Need:

- Birch logs
- Miter saw
- Tape measure
- Pencil
- Lag screws, brad nails, or wood glue
- Hanging brackets

**STEP 1**: Gather several evenly sized birch logs; you'll need enough logs to cut twenty segments measuring around 2 feet each.

**STEP 2**: Set a miter saw at an 18-degree angle and make sure the blade is sharp.

**STEP 3**: Begin by cutting one end of a birch log at an 18-degree angle.

**STEP 4**: Once the first cut is made, rotate the log clockwise, then turn it over 180 degrees. Make sure to rotate and then turn the log in this way, so the angled ends will match up later.

**STEP 5**: Measure 22¼ inches on the log from the outer edge of the angled cut, and mark with a pencil. Prepare to make the next cut by double-checking that it will produce an opposite-angled end on the log.

**STEP 6**: Make your second angled cut with the outer edge starting at the pencil mark. Number this log 1 with a pencil, and continue to number each log going forward. This will ensure that the pieces cut from the same stretch of log are matched up later for a snug fit.

**STEP 7**: Measure the newly cut log to be sure that the longest side is 22¼ inches.

**STEP 8**: Repeat steps 2 through 8 to cut nine more log segments, each one measuring 22¼ inches.

**STEP 9**: To create your inner ring, measure the shorter side of the logs you just cut. Use this measurement to determine the longest side of the next log set (this measurement will vary based on your log diameter).

**STEP 10**: Repeat steps 2 through 8 to cut ten segments for the interior ring of the wreath, using the measurement from step 10 for the longest side of each log.

**STEP 11**: Once all the log pieces have been cut, form the wreath by matching up the numbered pieces of each ring. Lay out the entire wreath on a flat surface to be sure that all angles fit tightly.

**STEP 12**: Use lag screws, brad nails, or wood glue to connect the logs, completing the wreath.

**STEP 13**: Use sturdy brackets to mount the wreath in your desired location.

## 4

*Design Ideas*

# Wreaths Beyond the Basics

Though the shape of a wreath is clearly defined, its potential for adaptability—
in both construction and purpose—is as endless as its circular silhouette. The
following pages look beyond the familiar uses of wreaths, and consider them
instead as innovative stand-ins for decorative elements throughout the home.

# Horizontal Wreaths

Reoriented to hang horizontally, wreaths serve as surprising installations. These impromptu chandeliers create a soft, botanical canopy that fosters a sense of intimacy when suspended in indoor and outdoor spaces alike. Paired with lights and candles, they also bathe the room—or patio— in a soft, golden glow. Turn to page 153 to learn how to create a glowing garden chandelier.

ABOVE: **A SPRING CHANDELIER** Lights and greens wrapped around the frame of a wreath hanger accent a dense circle of dried statice, studded with bay leaves and stems of sage.

OPPOSITE: **SUMMER CITRONELLA** Suspended from a three-pronged hook at the center of a patio pergola, a reindeer moss wreath is the focal point of an outdoor chandelier. The hook also supports a collection of glass votives hanging from lengths of jute twine, each one containing a practical citronella tea light for summer nights.

# A Wreath Gallery Wall

While a single wreath is a charming accent piece for the doorstep or mantel, a gathering of multiples makes a substantial impact. Dried, preserved, and faux options are best used to form the foundation of a wreath gallery, as they allow for a permanent display. Leave a few spaces for fresh wreaths, which can be swapped in to reflect the changing seasons. Here are some elements to keep in mind.

**MIXED MATERIALS:** Choose materials with varied colors and textures for visual interest, then unify the wall by repeating a few themes. Here, tight rings of dried flowers in eye-catching colors guide the viewer across the grouping. More subtle repeating themes include metal botanicals and dried vines, presenting a rich mix of materials that still feels purposeful and measured.

**SHAPE & SCALE:** Gather wreaths that vary widely in scale to create bold visual statements interspersed with smaller moments of interest. The repetition of circular silhouettes will help to unify wreaths of disparate sizes.

**OPEN SPACES:** Balance dense wreaths with airy designs that give the eye a chance to rest. In this instance, the loosely wrapped vine wreath at the center of the wall offsets nearby rings of metal roses and preserved ferns that have more substantial silhouettes.

**INTEGRATED ELEMENTS:** Connect the gallery to the overall décor of a space by adding tall objects that reach upward into the wall from the floor or a table.

# Baskets as Wreaths

Mounted on the wall, shallow baskets serve as ready-made bases for densely layered wreaths of seasonal finds. Their sturdy structure can support the weight of garlands, branches, lights, and even living bulbs.

ABOVE: **A WINTER BULB WREATH** The extra depth of a basket wreath welcomes unique, seasonal vignettes. Here, a nest of fresh moss holds newly sprouted paperwhites for a touch of winter green. The basket itself is concealed by a wild nest of twigs and rose hips, a stark juxtaposition for the tender green shoots within.

OPPOSTIE: **FALL LIGHTS AND LEAVES** An autumn wreath takes shape atop a chunky wicker basket, festooned with a mix of sorghum grass, eucalyptus, amaranthus, and pepperberry, then finished with a delicate strand of lights.

# Table Toppers

Wreaths serve as a ready-made centerpiece when laid flat on the table, offering up a full bouquet of seasonal stems. For a round table, try a pillar candle or pair of candlesticks at the center of a large wreath. For a long, rectangular table, place several smaller circlets in a line that reaches down its entire length.

LEFT: **GOOD FORM** A hollow metal form topped with taper cups (ours is from ShopTerrain.com) can be used to shape a centerpiece from any collection of natural materials, like this mix of wiry vines, clumps of moss, baby's breath, asparagus fern, and blown-out eggs.

OPPOSITE: **A SIMPLE TRANSFORMATION** A low-profile plant stand paired with a wreath of dried botanicals creates an instant centerpiece.

# Spotlight on Fall

*hearth & harvest*

———

Though the garden wanes as autumn arrives, these fleeting days put on a pageant that crowns the year's final harvests in color. Flame-bright leaves reach for the blue skies of clear, chilly afternoons, while a bounty of squashes, apples, and root vegetables fills orchard and field alike.

These natural signs of the changing seasons inspire cozy traditions. We carry pumpkins fresh from the patch to brighten the doorstep, and pluck the garden's final flowers in warm-hued bouquets to top the table. At the heart of these traditions is a desire to gather—to collect autumn's bounty for the sparse months ahead. This gathering instinct also extends to family and friends, who meet for celebrations of harvest and plenty as the days shorten.

# Dahlia Season with Floret Flowers

From coast to coast, the shoulder season between summer and fall brings bumper crops of blooms to American flower farms. When the dahlia harvest arrives in August and September, some of the year's most indisputably beautiful fields belong to Floret Flowers.

Based in Washington's Skagit Valley, Floret began as a farm and floral design studio. Today, they also offer seeds, bulbs, garden tools, and workshops for aspiring growers. Hoping to raise their family surrounded by nature, founder Erin Benzakein and her husband, Chris, moved to the farm from Seattle. They started with a huge vegetable garden but were pleasantly surprised by the incredible reactions they received when they started growing and sharing flowers. Seeing the impact that flowers can have on others piqued Erin's curiosity. She says, "I love that a bouquet can inspire tears, smiles, joy, or nostalgia. The recipient of my first bouquet teared up as she buried her face in the flowers, remembering happy childhood summers in her grandmother's garden. After that, I knew I had found my calling."

Every season at Floret has its standout blooms, starting with spring's ranunculus, anemones, and tulips. In early autumn, dahlias reign supreme. Erin says, "I'm often asked what my favorite flower is, and answering always feels like singling out a favorite child. In August and September, however, that question is always answered: dahlias. Dahlias, dahlias, dahlias."

Nearly ten thousand dahlias populate Floret's fields, and months of planning go into this rainbow-hued harvest. Dahlia tubers are planted two weeks after the last frost date, once the beds have been prepared with compost and fertilizer. Drip irrigation keeps up with the plants' high water demands, paired with a thick layer of mulch to insulate the new plantings. The mulch is pulled back a few weeks later, giving the new sprouts room to grow. Once the plants reach around 12 inches tall, they're snipped to increase stem count and overall stem length. Finally, each plant is staked in preparation for its bulky blooms.

After all this preparation, the harvest awaits. Erin says, "When dahlia harvest days arrive, we're all ready for the change of pace and welcome the monotonous, beautiful, steady task." She admits to dreaming of dahlias during the long stretches of harvest season, counting and bundling their stems before dropping them into water. Many days on the farm are spent in the dahlia fields from sunrise to sunset, gathering the vibrant flowers by the truckload.

Erin shares quite a few reasons to love these late bloomers. "While dahlias aren't a long-lasting cut flower, their brilliant blooms make up for their fleeting existence. They're easy to grow, come in a rainbow of colors, and are nearly unmatched in terms of flower production. What's not to love?"

Traditions

# Pennsylvania Pumpkin Auctions

Every autumn, in the rolling farmland of central Pennsylvania, mountains of pumpkins are auctioned fresh from the field. From Labor Day weekend through mid-October, when the weather is just right for outdoor auctions, farmers and buyers gather in search of the season's very best gourds.

Pumpkins and gourds are offered at produce auctions, which happen throughout the year. In early fall, they're mixed with other seasonal picks like cabbages and apples. Later in the season, the auctions focus more intensely on decorative pumpkins. At the height of pumpkin season, competition for the best varieties can be fierce!

The auction is a boisterous scene, filled with thousands of pumpkins, hundreds of bidders, and the singsong sound of auctioneers. At many auctions, Amish farmers from the region attend with huge wagons of produce.

Alongside classic orange carving pumpkins, heirloom varieties take center stage in shades of pink, gray, white, and pale green. In recent years, 'Jarrahdale' has been a consistent favorite thanks to its exceptional gray-green rind. Another star of the auction is 'Black Futsu,' a tiny ornamental squash that transforms from jet black to raspberry to gray as it ages. Unexpected treasures emerge each autumn at the auction, with previously unknown heirlooms and new cultivars expanding the pumpkin palette.

# Arrangements from the Wild

Through centuries and across cultures, botanical arrangements have marked moments of importance. In ancient Egypt, repeating displays of sacred lotus adorned tombs during burials. Thousands of years later, Victorians exchanged bouquets inspired by the "language of flowers," assigning each stem a meaning to convey elaborate messages. Today, arrangements still function as symbols—of joy and celebration, or loss and mourning—at occasions of all kinds, from Sunday dinners to weddings.

Although arrangements are a part of everyday life, they need not be everyday. The following pages look beyond the bouquet to discover the broader possibilities of arrangements, approached from a gardener's perspective where fresh, seasonal materials are prized over hothouse blooms. Traditional flowers and vases find a home alongside foraged branches and unconventional vessels. Planted specimens mingle with cut stems for unlikely displays of fleeting beauty. Centuries-old techniques from Japan inspire minimalist plantings in miniature. And in every display, no matter its style, the universal design principles of space, form, line, and texture are applied to create balanced, purposeful, and striking displays.

Whether planted, freshly cut, or an intriguing mix of the two, every design in this chapter reflects the key to our philosophy: a willingness to be adaptable and consider the wider possibilities of materials from the natural world. The arrangements that follow embrace budding branches, lush moss, tender saplings, and more unexpected finds alongside traditional cut flowers. Through these materials, each arrangement is tailored to celebrate the best of a particular season. With a resourceful approach and a designer's eye for detail, you can create truly beautiful botanical arrangements that reflect the dynamic landscape just outside your door.

PREVIOUS PAGES: Foraged elements from the early autumn landscape fill a meadow-inspired trough arrangement that serves as a conversation-starting dinner party centerpiece. (See page 224 for more on this arrangement.)

OPPOSITE: Look to unexpected places—sometimes quite literally outside your window—when surveying the wealth of natural elements at your disposal. An overgrowth of ivy, a budding tree, or a humble patch of herbs can offer options beyond traditional cut flowers for planning and creating arrangements.

# 1

*Look to Nature*

# Our Arrangement Philosophy

The art of arrangements adheres to just one firm rule: displays should highlight the best of the natural world. Aside from this dictate, the creative process is personal. When crafting an arrangement, think about what you haven't seen before, then experiment. Unusual combinations—of high and low, austere and abundant, cut and planted—surprise and delight the maker and viewer alike. A simple sapling is elevated when transformed into a bonsai-inspired tabletop planting, a gnarled branch gains architectural appeal in a stately vase, and foraged fall stems stand in for traditional flowers as a dinner party centerpiece. Be resourceful and survey the full breadth of the natural world to create intriguing and ever-changing arrangements throughout the seasons.

# Be Resourceful

When creating an arrangement, choosing your materials is the first and most important step. Each design should begin with an exploration of your own backyard. In many cases, the materials closest at hand are the most beautiful—and the most frequently overlooked.

For the enterprising designer, the abundant possibilities of the natural world extend beyond familiar garden flowers and foliage, offering colors, textures, and shapes not found in the cutting garden. Embrace the blooming branches and eager bulbs of early spring, the rangy wildflowers and sculptural seed heads of late summer, and the richly colored heirloom pumpkins of autumn. Branches in particular offer a wealth of possibilities, from the pastel blooms of forced tulip magnolia and drooping catkins of sawtooth oak, all the way to the vivid leaves of late-fall limbs. Plucked from field and forest, these wonderfully wild shapes transform an arrangement into a true reflection of nature, inviting the seasonal landscape into our homes and celebrations.

OPPOSITE: Keep a collection of long-lasting foraged elements like dried twigs, pinecones, pods, and mosses on hand as accent pieces. Some may be ready for use as is, while others require judicious preparation. Strip away foliage to expose unique pods or pull individual pinecones from a branch to create a textured topper.

ABOVE: Small foraged elements—leaves in saturated shades, tiny snippets of dripping vine, or dried seed heads—provide impactful pops of color and texture when mingled with more traditional fresh cuts.

# Curate Collections

When thoughtfully gathered, a grouping of miniature arrangements can be as impactful as a single large-scale bouquet or centerpiece. The key to a successful grouping is seeking and emphasizing its unifying elements, which guide the eye through the display to form a single arrangement, so be sure that each vessel features similar stems, colors, and textures to create a cohesive whole. Along with the stems and plants inside, vessels in similar or complementary materials help to shape a unified display.

LEFT: When lots of single stems and tiny foliage cuttings are on hand, gather a collection of bud vases for an effortless arrangement—for a cohesive look, choose glassware in similar shades.

OPPOSITE: A forest of miniature topiaries serves as an atypical arrangement for a sunny corner. The slender stems and top-heavy silhouettes of myrtle and lemon cypress topiaries are echoed by glossy aeonium; lower-profile succulents fill out the collection.

# 2

*Arrangements*
## Materials & Making

Every arrangement begins with two fundamental questions: what materials will it include, and what form will those materials take? While the questions are simple, a multitude of factors determines the answers—the season, the stems and plants on hand, the vessel, the space it will fill, and the occasion, just to name a few. A summer garden party demands fresh flowers in a bountiful bouquet, while the winter mantel calls for a simple pot of tiny leaves to introduce a subtle hint of green. The following pages take a closer look at three essential starting points for an arrangement: scale, vessels, and materials.

# Arrangements by Scale

The word *arrangement* may bring to mind a vase filled with fresh-cut flowers, but these versatile displays take on many more forms. Broadly, arrangements can be grouped into three categories based on scale—accents, centerpieces, and installations. No matter their size, arrangements capture the best of the natural world, and adapt its beauty to the location at hand.

## *Small Accents*

The most widely varied type of arrangement, this category includes the many kinds of smaller-scale displays that can brighten a living room, bedside table, or windowsill. Though accents are sometimes abundant bouquets, they most often serve as simpler moments of beauty and may take the form of fresh foliage in tiny jars, botanicals in found or repurposed vessels, and even terrariums.

Thanks to their myriad forms and compact sizes, accents are the perfect introduction to floral arranging. Simply drop your favorite flowers in a vase and place them in the entryway, atop a side table, or on the kitchen counter, and your arrangement is complete. As your confidence builds, this category offers room for innovation beyond the vase.

Petite plantings like this one (an understated combination of succulents and pine straw) can be placed anywhere you might display a vase of flowers, for a botanical touch that outlasts fresh cuts.

## Medium Centerpieces

The best type of conversation starter, centerpieces bring the table to life for festive gatherings. Traditionally, a centerpiece is designed in a long, narrow vessel that matches the silhouette of the table itself; however, these arrangements can take any number of shapes. Try scattering your favorite vases down the table with a few stems in each, or craft a living runner of fresh grasses directly on the tabletop.

This high-contrast centerpiece pairs the clean lines of a copper trough with an overgrown, early-summer planting. A trio of Japanese maple saplings is the focal point for the arrangement, surrounded by a wild collection of flowers and foliage. (This polished trough is a temporary home for its unusual inhabitants; the trees should be planted permanently in the ground as they grow larger.)

# *Grand Installations*

Installations fit the bill when an occasion requires an arrangement of truly grand scale. Adaptable and exceptional, these displays are fashioned to complement their environment and set the tone for an event. They offer intrepid designers the opportunity to reimagine the shapes and locations of arrangements, and to find new applications for abundant materials like seasonal foliage and lush blooms.

ABOVE: Inspired by the concept of a floral "brooch," an installation of cascading roses and color-washed leaves creates a lush canopy for an early-summer wedding. Delicate foliage, including burgundy-tinted pink dogwood and silver-backed *Elaeagnus*, echoes the lacy details of an antique temple, as well as the natural movement of the trees overhead.

OPPOSITE: A floating forest sets a captivating scene for a summer party, allowing guests to mingle among a grove of quaking aspen (*Populus tremuloides*). A rounded form at the base of each tree gives the effect of a "root-ball," filled with a collection of living plants and fresh-cut wildflowers.

# A Guide to Vessels

Vessels form the foundation for an arrangement and help to define the structure and style of your design. A tall vase may set a traditional tone and provide the necessary support for a collection of lofty branches, while a sleek trough offers contemporary style when planted with a centerpiece of colorful succulents.

1     **CLAY POTS:** A nod to garden tradition, tiny clay or terra-cotta pots make the perfect foundation for an arrangement of several small plantings. These rustic vessels let the plants inside take the spotlight, and offer a repeating silhouette that unifies indoor displays like this windowsill collection of society garlic (*Tulbaghia violacea*).

2     **URNS:** Like their larger counterparts in outdoor gardens, miniature urns bring classical appeal to arrangements. Try pairing them with simple, shaggy greens—like these mophead cypresses (*Chamaecyparis pisifera*)—for playful, high-low contrast.

3     **TROUGHS:** Sleek and simple, troughs are ideally shaped to serve as centerpieces for square and rectangular dining tables. They can be filled with an overflowing collection of fresh cuts or a long row of tiny plants.

4     **VASES:** When choosing from the dramatic range of vase sizes and silhouettes, consider the shape and materials that will best support your stems. A narrow mouth will keep a bouquet tightly bunched for a full appearance while a wide, weighty vessel ensures top-heavy flowering branches remain upright.

5     **TRAYS:** To create a unified display with a variety of arrangements, gather several small pots or vases from around the house atop a large tray. This collection makes a lively centerpiece and can be moved between spaces with ease.

6     **TERRARIUMS:** Lush arrangements of foliage plants become natural curiosities when displayed inside a glass terrarium, offering a unique view of roots and soil. Open-topped vessels allow taller plants to range outward, while cloches create a closed system that's ideal for moisture-loving specimens.

# Arrangement Components

Natural materials are the defining feature of an arrangement, and their selection is a crucial step when creating a new design. From wild branches and sprouting bulbs to fresh flowers and tiny succulents, the outside world offers up a bounty of materials for arrangements of every size and style.

## *Branches*

Perhaps the most remarkable material of all for arrangement design, branches offer statement-making scale, lush foliage, and bright blooms that enliven the home from the earliest days of spring to the waning weeks of late autumn. These sizable specimens also encourage us to explore the natural world, as we forage for the perfect branches to fill a vase or structure an installation. Flowering and leafing branches alike can be "forced" into early life as winter transitions to spring; learn more about this method and our favorite spring branches beginning on page 252. However, spring isn't the only season in which branches shine; throughout the year, they provide ample interest in the forms of foliage, berries, and fruit.

LEFT: Flowering trees— like this Japanese apricot studded in blush blossoms— are a source of abundant blooms when little else has emerged in the landscape.

OPPOSITE: Early-spring branches provide a study in contrast that makes for simple yet impactful arrangements, with craggy shapes accented by tender, unfurling leaves and blossoms.

# *Moss*

One of our favorite foraged finds, moss is a subtle component for arrangements that offers major impact. This is especially true during the lean winter months, when mosses are a rare source of natural greenery. Mosses are ideal for filling out the base of an arrangement, where they can conceal soil, small grower's pots, or floral frogs. They can also be used to keep top-heavy plants upright and conserve moisture for fresh-cut or living specimens. Be sure to collect just a few pieces of moss from a single colony; it is slow growing and will regenerate poorly if too much is removed from one area. If a mossy woodland is hard to find in your region, consider preserved options that match the color and texture of fresh mosses. Whether fresh or preserved, lush mosses capture the effect of "sous bois"—the forest floor—building understories of incredibly rich color and texture.

LEFT: A bed of moss at the base of an arrangement provides decorative support for plants or stems that can grow top heavy or unruly, like this collection of early-spring hyacinths.

OPPOSITE: Though most commonly found on the forest floor, moss can thrive on rocks, fallen logs, and living trees in moist, shady environments.

## Moss

Moss has a surprising secret—many of the most popular varieties aren't moss at all. Instead, they're lichens, liverworts, and bromeliads with a similar appearance and growth habit to those of moss.

**Clump moss:** This emerald-green moss takes its name from its clustered habit. Mist its surface at least twice a week to preserve its vibrant color.

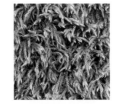

**Sheet moss:** Offering thick, carpet-like coverage, this versatile moss has a forest-green hue and a low-profile silhouette. Though exceptionally adaptable, it prefers low light and frequent misting.

**Reindeer moss:** The choice meal of reindeer, this cold-hardy, slow-growing lichen holds its color for extended periods when kept out of direct sunlight and regularly misted. It can also be dehydrated and dyed in a rainbow of colors.

**Spanish moss:** This Southern Gothic standby is an epiphyte rather than a moss, hanging in feathery chains from tree branches. Place in bright, indirect sunlight and mist to keep its surface moist.

## *Florals & Foliage*

Perhaps the most familiar components
for arrangements, fresh blooms provide an
instant burst of color that's hard to resist. (See
pages 202–203 for our favorite flowers to grow
in cutting gardens.) However, this category
encompasses a much wider range of materials than
the traditional bundle of blooms. Look beyond
ornamental plantings to find unique blossoms and
branches in the forest, shapely leaves in the herb
garden, sprouting bulbs in the spring meadow, and
vibrant fruits in the vegetable patch.

A traditional garden trug holds an ombré collection of lush,
freshly cut stems. From left to right, the bouquet includes
Dusty Miller (*Senecio*), *Fritillaria persica*, *Fritillaria meleagris*,
ranunculus, lilac (*Syringa*), *Fritillaria raddeana*, *Iris cristata*,
and tulips.

## Flowers for Cutting Gardens

Keep the ingredients for seasonal arrangements on hand by planting a cutting garden of exceptional flowers and foliage. The standout stems below are fantastic foundational pieces for crafting a wide variety of beautiful arrangements. We've divided our favorites into two categories: traditional stems for more formal bouquets, and wilder, meadow-inspired plants for informal arrangements.

### A FORMAL CUTTING GARDEN

**Anemone (*Anemone*):** Part of the ranunculus family, these perennials feature long, upright stems that are ideal for cut bouquets. Also known as windflowers, they range in color from white to saturated, poppylike red with sweetly rounded petals.

**Larkspur (*Delphinium*):** Tall spikes of saturated blue flowers make larkspur an impactful addition to summer arrangements. These showy flowers prefer mild climates with moist, cool summers.

**Dahlia (*Dahlia*):** The hardest part of planting dahlias is choosing just a few—with over 57,000 cultivars, the genus is exceptionally diverse. Rich in pigment and texture, they range from dainty 2-inch blooms to giant "dinner plate" varieties.

**Lisianthus (*Eustoma grandiflorum*):** A unique alternative to roses, elegantly ruffled lisianthus is well suited to formal arrangements and is available in an array of cool tones.

**English rose (*Rosa*):** English roses provide an excellent introduction to rose cultivation, known for their abundant blooms, strong fragrance, and relatively simple care requirements.

**Peony (*Paeonia*):** Festooned with lush, velvety petals, peonies are the perfect blooms for a monoculture bouquet. Later in the season, their star-shaped pods can be added to dried arrangements.

**Foxglove (*Digitalis*):** Tall spikes of vivid blooms make this flower a favorite for cottage garden arrangements. The clustered, tubular flowers can range in color from white and yellow to pink and purple.

**Ranunculus (*Ranunculus*):** Ranunculus offer straight stems and a long vase life. Their abundant blooms feature dense layers of delicate petals for a roselike appearance, ranging in color from pure white to splashy picotee.

**Hollyhock (*Alcea*):** Easy to grow from seed, these popular ornamentals feature brightly hued blooms (from bright white to deep burgundy) on towering stems.

**Scabiosa (*Scabiosa*):** Also known as pincushion flowers, these low-maintenance blooms are a part of the honeysuckle family. A popular pick for butterfly gardens, they will produce pastel flowers from spring through first frost.

## AN INFORMAL CUTTING GARDEN

**Amaranth (*Amaranthus*)**: The fuzzy, drooping flowers of amaranth lend striking texture and movement to a centerpiece or installation.

**Marguerite daisy (*Argyranthemum frutescens*)**: This small, shrublike perennial blooms best in cool weather. Pink or white petals are paired with a chartreuse center for a pop of color in spring or autumn bouquets.

**Aster (*Aster*)**: These daisylike perennials offer remarkable diversity in color and size, with around 180 species in cultivation. Asters bring a fresh wave of blooms to the garden in late summer.

**Mountain mint (*Pycnanthemum virginianum*)**: Small, silver-green leaves make mountain mint a top pick for dainty foliage to accent cut florals and fill out a bouquet; it also attracts pollinators to the garden.

**Cornflower (*Centaurea cyanus*)**: Also known as bachelor's buttons, these cheerful members of the aster family are native to Europe. Cornflowers most commonly produce saturated blue flowers atop gray-green stems.

**Nigella (*Nigella damascena*)**: Also known as love-in-a-mist, nigella is available in white, blue, purple, and pink shades. Its nickname is derived from its fennel-like foliage, which surrounds each bloom in a fine mist.

**Goldenrod (*Solidago*)**: A common sight in wild meadows, the flashy flower heads of goldenrod bring saturated shades of yellow to freshly cut bouquets in late summer and early autumn.

**Queen Anne's lace (*Daucus carota*)**: Also known as wild carrot, Queen Anne's lace is a common summer sight. Its umbels of tiny flowers are most often white, but a few varieties offer up striking, chocolate-brown blooms.

**Joe-pye weed (*Eutrochium purpureum*)**: A towering addition to the garden, standard varieties of joe-pye weed can reach up to 7 feet in height. Its large purple flowers emerge in late summer, continuing through early fall.

**Sorghum (*Sorghum vulgare*)**: Most often cultivated as an edible grain, sorghum is also a fantastic ornamental thanks to its large plumelike seed heads. Excellent for fresh or dried use, it's available in a variety of warm, earthy tones.

# Succulents

For arrangements that will outlast cut stems, consider using living options—including vivid succulents and tiny annuals—to create small-scale planted arrangements. A planted arrangement offers all the color and texture of a freshly cut bouquet, with added longevity once it takes root. Succulents are a particularly low-maintenance option for living arrangements, offering lots of visual impact with minimal care.

A mixed collection of echeveria, sedum, and stonecrops reveals the astonishing spectrum of colors and textures offered by succulents. The high-contrast combination shown here comes to life with frosty green accents in a field of intense reds and near-black purples.

## Jewel-Tone Succulents

Succulents benefit from long days of sunbathing, which bring out their brightest colors: deep reds, warm oranges, and shocking pinks. The varieties below are just a few of the many specimens that could be combined to create a jewel-tone arrangement.

*Echeveria:* Native to semidesert regions of Central and South America, *Echeveria* are characterized by symmetrical rosettes of broad, fleshy leaves. Outstanding options for color include rosy 'Perle von Nürnberg' and lavender 'Afterglow,' which features leaves edged in shocking pink.

*Graptopetalum pachyphyllum:* This low-profile perennial grows in large colonies. Its rosettes of glaucous leaves are topped by tiny yellow flowers with pointed petals. In bright sun, the silver-gray foliage takes on a reddish tint.

*Jovibarba hirta:* A form of hens and chicks, *Jovibarba hirta* is also commonly called "rollers." The red-tinted mother rosette sends the "chicks" up high on brittle stems that break easily, rolling the babies away to root.

*Kalanchoe thyrsiflora:* Commonly known as "paddle plant," "flapjack plant," or "desert cabbage," this South African native produces pink-edged leaves when grown in bright sunlight. Its rounded paddles provide the backdrop for a tall spike of fragrant yellow flowers in spring.

**Sedum:** Many varieties of these low-profile succulents are rich in color. *Sedum sieboldii* 'Mediovariegatum' (syn. *Hylotelephium sieboldii*) features leaves in yellow, white, and pale blue. *Sedum rubrotinctum* 'Aurora' (nicknamed "pink jelly beans") is another cheerfully colored cultivar with beadlike leaves in pink and cream.

# Faux & Forever

Though most arrangements celebrate the freshness of natural materials, some occasions call for a longer-lasting display. When living flowers and foliage aren't available, or if they would wilt quickly under adverse conditions, faux and dried stems can step in. For the perfect trompe l'oeil effect, try mixing faux stems with fresh or dried natural elements.

ABOVE: Brimming with fall foliage, flowers, and berries, this candlelit centerpiece deserves a second look: every stem is faux.

OPPOSITE: A collection of vibrant green stems showcases the diversity and quality of modern faux botanicals. This grouping includes grasses, Queen Anne's lace, *Sorbus*, *Kerria japonica*, ranunculus, and more.

# Five Key Concepts for Arrangement Design

Crafting an arrangement is ultimately a creative pursuit, dictated by what's freshest in the world outside. However, a few guiding principles will help you shape a well-structured arrangement that suits the season, location, and occasion at hand.

**1. UNITY:** When selecting materials, consider the color palette of the arrangement as a whole. Choose stems in complementary shades and distribute the colors evenly, especially in a larger arrangement. Seasonality also serves as a unifying factor; the bright flowers of goldenrod and helenium are natural companions for foraged fall foliage, while hothouse roses would be an incongruous fit.

**2. REPETITION:** Select materials with repeating colors, textures, and shapes that will appear consistently throughout the arrangement. Repetition is an especially important consideration for displays made up of multiple small-scale arrangements, like a grouping of bud vases filled with miniature bouquets. The recurring elements work to guide the eye through the collection, creating a cohesive display.

**3. BALANCE:** For ample weight and presence, choose medium-mass stems for the majority of the arrangement. (Exceptions to this arise in purposefully spare styles like ikebana; see page 239.) Taller, upright stems and smaller, spreading specimens can then be selected as accent pieces.

**4. EMPHASIS:** Though unity, repetition, and balance work together to create a cohesive arrangement, there's still room to showcase impactful stems. An oversize branch, vivid bloom, or specimen with a remarkable silhouette should serve as the focal point of your arrangement, highlighting key colors and textures and creating a dynamic display.

**5. PLACEMENT:** If grouping vessels, place the tallest ones at the back and the shortest at the front. Not only does this guarantee that all components are seen, it hides any unsightly stems among the taller specimens. Placement should also take into account where an arrangement will be displayed; tall branches are the perfect point of interest for a high-ceilinged entryway but might hinder conversation at the center of the table.

Multihued ranunculus blooms anchor a strikingly spare arrangement, centered around a white tree peony. Dry, windswept leaves serve as a foraged backdrop, while repeating colors and textures unify the display: the ranunculus introduce pink and yellow tones that reappear in the peony, and their ruffled edges are echoed in the curling leaves.

# 3

*Unexpected Blooms*

# Eight Arrangement Projects

Truly exceptional arrangements come to life when several elements work in tandem: beautiful materials, thoughtfully selected vessels, complementary locations, and notable occasions. The following pages take a closer look at eight exceptional displays to discover how their styles and settings combine for a design that's far more than the sum of its parts. These detailed explorations also offer step-by-step instructions for re-creating the look in your own home. Each one tells a story, from romantic floral installations at a garden wedding to ripe fruits and rustling grasses atop the table for a harvest feast.

# A Lights & Leaves Garland

Made from intricate layers of glowing lights and living plants, a simple garland transforms into an unexpected arrangement that brightens outdoor evenings. A luminous strand of old-fashioned globe lights is the perfect counterpoint to gathering twilight, especially when accented by a wild mix of preserved ferns, air plants, dried grapevine, and worn metal leaves. This glowing arrangement is an easy way to illuminate the porch or doorstep in summer and early autumn. (See page 210 for another view of this garland.)

## What You'll Need:
- Malleable vine, such as grapevine
- Garden snips
- 1 strand of globe lights
- Floral wire
- Wire snips
- Metal foliage garland (ours came from ShopTerrain.com)
- Preserved foliage, such as ferns (learn to preserve botanicals with glycerin on page 135)
- Air plants

**STEP 1:** Cut a length of vine to match the length of your light strand. Wind the vine loosely around the light strand, using floral wire to secure it to the cord and letting some tendrils hang free for a more natural look.

**STEP 2:** Weave the metal garland through the lights and vine, using floral wire to fasten it as needed. Avoid wrapping the metal strand tightly around the cord or light sockets.

**STEP 3:** Add sprigs of preserved foliage to the garland, using wire or twine as needed.

**STEP 4:** Top off the strand with a few air plants, secured with floral wire. The air plants can remain on the garland until temperatures drop below 50°F, at which point they should be replaced with dried and faux stems.

# An Early Spring Pot-et-Fleur

*Pot-et-fleur*, literally translated to "pot and flower," is a style of floral arranging that became fashionable during the Victorian era. Combining cut flowers with potted plants was considered both beautiful and economical, as it allowed a single arrangement to be reused when spent stems were replaced with fresh flowers.

Crafted in celebration of winter's end, this design brings the art of pot-et-fleur to the modern era. Two orchids are planted in an understated terra-cotta urn that counterbalances their elevated blooms, then surrounded by budding poplar branches, ferns, and more fresh cuts.

## What You'll Need:

- Footed terra-cotta urn
- Waterproof liner (plastic pot or sheeting)
- *Oncidium* orchid, in grower's pot
- *Cypripedium* (lady's slipper) orchid, in grower's pot
- Floral foam
- Vessel for soaking the foam
- Garden snips
- Fresh-cut poplar branches
- Fresh-cut plumosa fern
- Fresh-cut Rex begonia leaves
- Fresh-cut clematis
- Fresh-cut sweet pea
- Fresh-cut anthurium
- Fresh-cut scabiosa
- Floral water tubes (also known as water picks)

**STEP 1:** Line the urn with a waterproof material—plastic sheeting or a plastic pot of the same dimensions is ideal.

**STEP 2:** Place the orchids, still in their grower's pots, inside the lined urn. Allow the *Oncidium* blooms to spill over one side of the urn for asymmetry and movement.

**STEP 3:** Cut the floral foam to size. Choose a vessel large enough to submerge the floral foam in and fill it with water. Place the foam in the vessel and let it soak gradually (don't push it down), until it turns dark green and sinks below the waterline.

**STEP 4:** Tuck pieces of foam around the orchid pots, creating a layer that covers the bottom of the urn. This will hold the pots in place while providing support and hydration for the fresh-cut stems.

**STEP 5:** Prep the fresh cuts. Remove blooms and leaves that are past their prime. Use sharp garden snips to trim stems to the appropriate size, and make sure every stem gets a fresh snip at its base immediately before going into the foam.

**STEP 6:** Begin inserting the stems into the floral foam. Start with the larger poplar branches, inserting them upright at an angle that mirrors the architectural *Oncidium* bloom. Cluster the ferns near the base of the arrangement for an airy, trailing silhouette.

**STEP 7:** Continue adding fresh cuts until the orchid pots and foam are fully concealed. Stems that are too delicate to be inserted directly into the floral foam can be placed in individual water tubes before insertion. These tubes can be anchored in the peripheral soil of the potted plants to fill out the arrangement.

**STEP 8:** Water to replenish moisture in the soil and floral foam as needed to prolong the life of the arrangement. Replace spent stems with fresh ones as needed. Care for the potted orchids as normal until you're ready to disassemble the arrangement.

# An Overflowing Summer Urn

Welcoming guests to an open-air wedding reception, this dramatic bouquet sets a celebratory yet refined tone, with structural foraged elements punctuated by more diaphanous florals. Deep green branches find striking counterpoints in a refreshing pastel palette of pale silvers and pinks. A compact metal pot supports the oversize botanicals, emphasizing their wild and dramatic shape in a nod to the lush landscape of late summer.

## What You'll Need:

- Metal pot or vase
- Waterproof liner (plastic insert or sheeting)
- Floral foam
- Vessel for soaking the foam
- Garden snips
- Acacia
- Russian olive branches
- Knotweed
- Pampas grass
- Pink sedum
- Grevillea
- Dahlias
- Hydrangea
- White larkspur

**STEP 1**: Line your pot with a plastic insert or sheeting. This will prevent leakage and rust, and keep the metal from affecting the pH levels in the water.

**STEP 2**: Cut a piece of floral foam to size and let it soak in a vessel filled with water (don't push it down), until it turns dark green and sinks below the waterline. Place the piece in the base of the pot.

**STEP 3**: Use sharp garden snips to trim stems to the appropriate size, and make sure every stem gets a fresh snip at its base immediately before going into the foam. Remove blooms and leaves that are past their prime, as well as any foliage that will be underwater in the vessel.

**STEP 4**: Start by anchoring the larger branches (acacia, Russian olive, knotweed) upright in the floral foam. Be sure to insert them at different angles to achieve an effortless, organic shape.

**STEP 5**: Begin to fill in the arrangement with textural greens, grasses, and florals around the large branches, allowing the shape to fan outward atop the metal pot. Reserve some of the dahlias, hydrangea, and larkspur for the next step.

**STEP 6**: Add a cluster of dahlias, hydrangea, and larkspur near the center of the bouquet to create a focal point with lots of brightness and contrast.

**STEP 7**: Fill the vase with fresh, cool water.

### HOW TO KEEP FRESH CUTS FRESH

Extend the life of fresh flowers and foliage with these simple care techniques.

- Fill your vessel with cold water, and choose a cool area away from direct sunlight to display the arrangement.
- Give the stems a fresh snip at the base and change the water every two or three days to avoid bacteria growth.
- Use flower food, which contains sugar to feed cut stems and a bactericide to keep the water fresher. It's easiest to purchase preportioned packets and add one each time you change the water. (Note: a few types of blooms should not be given any type of food, and bulbs need specially formulated foods, so check the requirements for each type of stem in a bouquet.)

# A Tabletop Succulent Kokedama

Derived from the *Nearai* and *Kusamono* styles of bonsai, *kokedama* are miniature plantings that sprout from moss-wrapped balls of soil. In the Nearai tradition, a planting is grown in a compact pot until the vessel fills with roots; the root-ball is then removed from the pot and the entire planting is showcased on a flat tray. Kokedama capture the effect with a sphere of soil and moss, in which plants can take root. Much easier to cultivate than traditional bonsai, these mossy marvels were originally displayed on altarlike platforms. Today, the tiny arrangements work well on tabletops, where they serve as living centerpieces.

Succulents are ideal specimens for a kokedama arrangement, thanks to their hardy nature and limited water needs. Perch small-scale succulent kokedama inside unexpected objects—like widemouthed vases, votive cups, or petite bowls—for a fresh alternative to the centerpiece bouquet.

## What You'll Need:
- Succulents
- Potting soil (optional)
- Sheet moss
- Garden snips
- Clear fishing line or garden twine
- Widemouthed vase or small bowl

**STEP 1:** Choose your succulent. If your plant is already in soil, remove it from the pot or garden bed, leaving enough soil to fully cover its roots. Use your thumbs to pat down soil around the roots, forming a sphere. Incorporate additional soil if needed to create a better growing area.

**STEP 2:** Cut a piece of moss that will completely cover the ball of soil. Soak the moss in water and drain.

**STEP 3:** Place the ball of soil in the center of the sheet moss, with the mossy side facing away from the soil. Wrap the root-ball completely, pressing gently to make sure it stays together.

**STEP 4:** Begin wrapping the moss ball with fishing line or twine (use fishing line if you'd like the appearance of a solid moss surface, or twine for a more rustic look). Wrap snugly and crisscross the strand, keeping in mind that this helps the ball maintain its shape. When you've finished wrapping, tie the ends of the strand together in a strong knot.

**STEP 5:** Choose a vase, bowl, or other vessel and place the completed kokedama inside for display.

**STEP 6:** Check your kokedama's weight to determine when it needs water; when dry, it will feel very light. To water, fill a bowl with water, then submerge the moss ball and watch for bubbles. When you no longer see bubbles, it's fully soaked. Gently squeeze out excess liquid and drain in the sink.

# A Dramatic Summer Centerpiece

Created for a dinner celebrating the late-summer harvest, this multivessel centerpiece reflects the abundance of the season. Dark botanicals inspired by some of summer's most dramatic specimens unify a palette of deep purples, soft pinks, and sunset oranges, offset with grasses in muted tones that hint at the imminent arrival of autumn. Plucked fresh from the garden, the grasses are arranged directly on the table to create a natural runner, which holds a collection of tiny vases and richly colored bouquets to create a lush, layered look.

**What You'll Need:**
- Garden snips
- Fresh ornamental grasses
- Multiple bud vases
- Multiple full-size vases
- Rose hips
- Smoke bush
- Ornamental stones
- Dahlias
- Sunflowers
- Pink echinacea
- Andromeda
- Queen Anne's lace
- Oak leaf hydrangea

**STEP 1:** Cut a variety of ornamental grasses using garden snips. Use them to create a textured "runner" by placing them down the center of the table, directly on the tablecloth.

**STEP 2:** Choose your bud vases and full-size vases. The exact number will be determined by the size of the table. For a cohesive look, stick to a single material—all pottery, all glass, all silver—and complementary colors.

**STEP 3:** Create bouquets to match the scale of the bud vases, using smaller stems such as rose hips and sprigs of smoke bush. Give each stem a fresh snip at the base, remove blooms and leaves that are past their prime, as well as any that would be underwater, and place the small bouquets in the bud vases with fresh, cool water.

**STEP 4:** Fill the bottom of the full-size vases with a layer of ornamental stones, then add fresh, cool water.

**STEP 5:** Create bouquets to match the scale of the full-size vases (following the prep instructions in step 3) with dahlias, sunflowers, and echinacea as focal points. Add sprays of ornamental grass for height, and andromeda for a draping silhouette at the periphery of each bouquet. Give each stem a fresh cut at the base.

**STEP 6:** Scatter the vases down the length of the table, nestling them into the grass runner. See page 216 for advice on prolonging the life of your arrangements.

# A Woodland Wedding Arch

Setting the scene for a deep-woods wedding in the Pocono Mountains, this wild installation on a timber pavilion mirrors the overgrowth of summer's end in the surrounding landscape. Lush foliage makes the installation a graceful extension of the environs, while a magical array of flowers sets it apart from its surroundings, defining the space for an intimate ceremony.

Unpruned swaths of Russian olive (*Elaeagnus angustifolia*), eucalyptus, and honeysuckle form the base of the bohemian-style arrangement, accented with a textural swirl of foraged knotweed and an eclectic mix of florals including panicled hydrangea (*Hydrangea paniculata*), garden roses, astilbe, sedum, and asclepias.

## What You'll Need:

- Floral foam
- Vessel for soaking the foam
- Zip ties
- Vinyl-coated chicken wire
- Garden snips
- Russian olive branches
- Honeysuckle vine
- Eucalyptus
- Floral wire
- Wire snips
- Astilbe
- Sedum
- Asclepias
- Knotweed
- Panicled hydrangea
- Garden roses

**STEP 1:** Choose a vessel large enough to submerge the floral foam and fill it with water. Place the foam in the vessel and let it soak gradually (don't push it down), until it turns dark green and sinks below the waterline.

**STEP 2:** Locate a stable section of the structure and use zip ties to attach a few blocks of presoaked floral foam to the beams. This will provide hydration and a base to anchor the more delicate florals.

**STEP 3:** Use the chicken wire to create a cage around the foam and a broader section of the surrounding beam, attaching it to the beam with zip ties. This will support the larger branches and allow them to be tucked in from any angle.

**STEP 4:** Use sharp garden snips to trim the large sturdy branches (Russian olive, honeysuckle, eucalyptus) to the appropriate size, and start tucking them into the chicken-wire cage. Place the base of each branch near the center of the cage, letting the branches spray outward to create an asymmetrical shape for drama and movement. Use loops of floral wire to secure them to the cage for additional support, if needed.

**STEP 5:** Once the large branches are in place, trim and add the more delicate fresh cuts (astilbe, sedum, asclepias, knotweed) to fill out the shape of the arrangement. Anchor the stems into the floral foam at the center of the wire cage, and use floral wire as needed for support and shaping.

**STEP 6:** Cluster the largest blooms (hydrangea, garden roses) near the center of the arrangement to create a colorful focal point, inserting the stems into the floral foam. Though this arrangement is intended for temporary display, you can prolong the life of the botanicals by using a watering can or gentle hose to moisten the foam and fresh cuts as needed.

# A Harvest Meadow Table

The centerpiece for an elegant autumn dinner, this expansive trough is filled with stems gathered fresh from the garden and meadow. Statement botanicals including architectural *Verbena bonariensis* and glossy clusters of pokeberries showcase the abundance of foraged finds available in autumn. Color-splashed stems of coleus and goldenrod further highlight the diversity of fall foliage plants, their bright hues contrasting with cool blue atlas cedar. Weathered iron fern fronds are scattered throughout the fresh stems for a play on scale; their rustic texture also serves as a counterpoint to the lush botanicals.

## What You'll Need:

- Galvanized metal trough(s)
- Waterproof liner (plastic trough insert or sheeting)
- Floral foam
- Vessel for soaking the foam
- Garden snips
- Blue atlas cedar
- Goldenrod
- Coleus
- Hibiscus
- *Verbena bonariensis*
- Pennycress
- Artemisia
- Celosia
- Strawflower
- Pokeweed
- Grasses
- Weathered iron leaves

**STEP 1:** Select a trough that spans the full length of your table, or line up multiple troughs if needed. If using multiples, think of them as one large vessel when placing the stems within your arrangement.

**STEP 2:** Line the trough with a plastic insert or sheeting to avoid leakage onto the table, and to prevent the metal from affecting the pH levels in the water.

**STEP 3:** Soak blocks of floral foam in a vessel filled with water; let them soak gradually (don't push them down), until they turn dark green and sink below the waterline. Place blocks of floral foam end to end inside the trough, until the entire length of the trough is covered.

**STEP 4:** Prep the fresh cuts. Remove blooms and leaves that are past their prime. Use sharp garden snips to trim stems to the appropriate size, and make sure every stem gets a fresh snip at its base immediately before going into the foam.

**STEP 5:** Begin inserting the stems into the floral foam. Start with the largest botanicals to create focal points and work downward in size to the smallest. As you arrange, consider ways to highlight the natural movement of each element, since guests will be up close and personal with the display. For example, let tall plumes of grass stand up from the center of the trough, or let bunches of pokeberries cascade over the sides.

**STEP 6:** Survey the trough as a whole to make sure all the floral foam is covered and no gaps are apparent. Insert additional fresh cuts as needed.

**STEP 7:** Tuck the iron leaves throughout the arrangement to serve as accent pieces. Add water to the vessel regularly to keep the foam moist and prolong the life of the arrangement. Replace spent stems with fresh ones as needed.

# An Impossible Orchid Planting

During the seventeenth and eighteenth centuries, a trend emerged in the work of Dutch painters: the impossible bouquet. The imaginary subject of a still life, an impossible bouquet could exist only on canvas because the flowers it contained would never bloom at the same time. Today, nearly any cut flower can be sourced at any time, making it possible to realize these once-imaginary bouquets. However, the idea of an "impossible" arrangement survives in unlikely planted combinations—like this lush green bowl designed for temporary display. The impermanence of this arrangement makes its beauty all the more remarkable, so it's the perfect home accent for a late-winter celebration.

A high-contrast *Miltonia* orchid serves as the centerpiece for this impossible arrangement. Also known as pansy orchids, *Miltonia* orchids resemble a classic spring bloom, making them the perfect pick for winter, a preview for the season ahead. Finicky orchids are ill suited for permanent planting with heat-loving succulents, but a clever technique helps this short-term planting thrive.

## What You'll Need:

- Large, shallow bowl planter
- *Miltonia* orchid, in grower's pot
- Jasmine, in grower's pot
- *Echeveria pulvinata* Devotion, in grower's pot
- *Echeveria gibbiflora* Summer Joy, in grower's pot
- Fresh clump or sheet moss

**STEP 1:** Place the plants inside the bowl, still inside their plastic grower's pots from the nursery. Situate the orchid at the center of the bowl, then disperse the jasmine and echeveria around it. Keeping the plants in their individual vessels makes it simple to take apart this temporary arrangement.

**STEP 2:** Once the plants are in place, fill in the gaps between each pot with a layer of moss. Continue adding moss until the pots are fully concealed, filling in around the base of each plant.

**STEP 3:** After a few days of display, remove the moss and place each plant in an individual vessel for proper care.

# 4

*Design Ideas*

# Arrangements Beyond the Basics

Constance Spry, longtime florist to Great Britain's royal family, prescribed a decidedly personal approach to floral arranging: "Do whatever you please," she declared. "Follow your own star; be original if you want to be and don't if you don't want to be. Just be natural and gay and light-hearted and pretty and simple and overflowing and general and baroque and bare and austere and stylized and wild and daring and conservative, and learn and learn and learn. Open your mind to every form of beauty."

Spry's advice perfectly captures the imaginative spirit of arrangements and guides the collection of design ideas that follow—from simple, slender twigs rooted in water to a spectacular tabletop of living sedum. Each one is open to adaptation with your favorite blooms of the moment.

# Roots in Glass

Showcasing roots in a transparent glass vessel makes for a striking and unexpected arrangement. Surprisingly graceful and rarely seen, the growing roots become tiny sculptures when suspended in clean water.

The rise of this minimalist cultivation style can be traced to Northern Europe—Sweden in particular—where natural growers experimented with swapping soil for nutrient-rich water. They discovered that this approach takes up less space than traditional rooting yet yields especially prolific results.

A wide variety of plants can be rooted in glass with minimal effort. Good choices include household herbs like mint, basil, rosemary, and sage; familiar plants like geranium, peace lily, philodendron, and ivy; and small trees or saplings. When choosing a vessel, look for transparent glass, a thin neck to support the plant's stem, and a bulbous bottom to permit root growth. When rooting larger branches, also select a vessel that's weighty enough to support the stems without toppling over.

LEFT: **A NEW VIEW** These impactful displays can be scaled to suit any space; try a single large vessel with a stem sized to match, or a grouping of several tiny root systems elevated on miniature plant stands.

OPPOSITE: **WINTER LIGHT** The combination of light-catching glass and fresh green stems is especially striking as winter transitions to spring, when signs of growth are most prized.

# Living Succulent Centerpieces

On the hottest days of summer, consider alternatives to traditional fresh cuts when creating tabletop arrangements. Planted succulents provide a resilient, easy-to-grow option for small-scale plantings that are rich in color and texture, no flowers required. (See pages 234–236 for two ways to grow your own succulents for planted arrangements.)

OPPOSITE: **LONG TROUGHS** Low-profile troughs make the perfect home for a tabletop succulent centerpiece, with lots of room for collections of diverse and colorful specimens. They can be kept on the patio table throughout the warmer months and transferred to the home when an indoor display is needed.

ABOVE: **LOW BOWLS** Succulent gardens planted in shallow bowls are a sleek and contemporary centerpiece option. These dense arrangements are compact in scale, making them ideal for smaller settings or times when tabletop space is at a premium. Low-profile shapes like this rough-hewn bowl also allow conversation to flow freely.

# *Propagating Succulents*

It's surprisingly simple to cultivate your own succulents for use in planted arrangements. In just a few weeks, you'll be able to grow a fresh crop of your favorite specimens.

## Stage 1: Gather Your Plant Material

To start the propagation process, you'll first need to collect plant material from the succulents you'd like to grow. This can be done via division or offsets.

**DIVISION:** This technique, in which cuttings are used to sprout new succulents, is ideal if you have rosette-shaped succulents, like *Echeveria* or *Graptopetalum,* that have become leggy. To begin, carefully remove any leaves on the stem below the rosette—wiggle them gently from side to side and keep the base of the leaf intact. Once all the leaves have been removed, use shears to snip the rosette, leaving a short stem attached. Allow the cuttings (leaves and rosettes) to dry for a few days in an empty tray until the raw ends have calloused.

**OFFSETS:** Many species of succulents—like aloe or hens and chicks—produce offsets, or small plants that grow at the base of the main specimen. Once an offset has grown for two to three weeks, check for root development and remove it from the main stem with a sharp knife or snips. Be careful to avoid damaging any roots that have already emerged. As above, allow the offsets to dry and form a callous over any open areas. (As a bonus, removing offsets improves the health of your existing succulents, focusing energy on the growth of the main plant.)

LEFT: **DIVISION** A tiny new succulent sprouts from the base of its "parent" leaf. As its roots develop, the leaf will wither and be ready for removal before the new succulent is planted.

OPPOSITE: **ROOTING IN WATER** Root your succulent in a water-filled glass vessel for an unusual botanical display. Top off the water as needed to keep the roots covered, and periodically refill the vase with fresh water.

## Stage 2: Rooting

Once the cuttings or offsets have calloused, there are two methods for developing their roots. The first is in water: rest them on the rim of a glass of water, with the end of the stem or existing roots just above the water's surface. Choose a sunny spot for your glass. Over time, roots will develop and reach toward the water (see photo on preceding page). Once roots are established, the new succulent can continue to live with the roots submerged in water, or be replanted in soil.

Another propagation method, rooting in stone, requires just a tray of gravel, a splash of water, and a bit of patience. Here's how to do it.

**STEP 1:** Fill a shallow tray with a drainage medium like gravel or Growstone.

**STEP 2:** Pour water over the stones just until the bottom of the tray is covered. This will force the succulents' roots to stretch toward the water.

**STEP 3:** Situate the cuttings and leaves among the stones. Anchor them deeply enough to keep them in place, but don't let them touch the water.

**STEP 4:** Place the tray in direct sunlight and watch for new growth to appear (four to six weeks after planting), adding water as needed. Once the cuttings have established new roots, they can be transplanted into soil.

ROOTING IN SOIL: Shown here, a tray featuring a collection of jewel-tone succulents developing roots, including *Aeonium* spp. (top left), *Echeveria* spp. (center), and *Kalanchoe thysiflora* (lower right).

# The Art of Ikebana

Airy and elegant, arrangements inspired by the Japanese floral school of ikebana are the perfect way to highlight and appreciate remarkable stems. Defined by its dedication to restraint and simplicity, the Japanese floral school of ikebana dates back more than a thousand years. *Ikebana* translates to "living flowers"; the practice is also known as *kadō,* meaning "way of flowers." Beginning with seventh-century floral altar offerings, this style of arranging has grown to include over a thousand schools of design. In the fifteenth century, Japanese painter Sōami proposed that ikebana arrangements should represent three elements: heaven, human, and earth. This remains the guiding principle of the craft today.

Sōami's contemplation of such lofty elements is key to understanding ikebana: more than a decorative art, it's also a meditative, disciplined, and spiritual practice. Sōfu Teshigahara, founder of the Sōgetsu School, said, "In ikebana, the flowers are imbued with a human meaning." Many arrangements are built around three focal plants, showcasing the artist's interpretation of Sōami's three principles. The spiritual elements of ikebana are equal to its aesthetics for many practitioners; some make their arrangements in silence, using the time for reflection and appreciation of beauty.

Negative space is key for ikebana arrangements, whose creators forgo abundant blooms in order to highlight exceptional components and subtle details. As seen in this collection of winter branches and blooms, ikebana also emphasizes different lengths and layers, so each stem can be viewed in isolation or with its companions. Varied elements also provide points of contrast and contemplation, as when juxtaposing fresh and dried stems and large leaves and wispy blades.

Centered on arching magnolia branches, this winter ikebana showcases fresh begonia, ranunculus, and cyclamen alongside dried ferns and miscanthus. A wire floral frog inside the bowl provides support, allowing each stem to lean the way it would inherently grow to create natural movement. This spare arrangement will last longer than a full bouquet; stems can easily be plucked out or replaced as they fade.

# Tiny Tabletop Leaves

In lieu of a more traditional centerpiece, collect a variety of tiny potted plants with unique foliage to dress the table. Delicate, leafy greens and intricate, rosette-shaped succulents are ideal for these living arrangements; their complex textures and compact shapes invite closer observation from those gathered at the table. The key to this look is the charming size of each planting; each pot should be small enough to hold in the palm of your hand.

ABOVE: **CALOCEPHALUS** Part of the aster family, slender *Calocephalus* offers tabletop impact when its silver-green leaves are presented against a backdrop of dark stone.

LEFT: **ECHEVERIA** Overflowing with a crop of rosette-shaped echeveria, a tiny potted arrangement brings lots of texture to the table.

**CREEPING MAZUS** The shapely leaves and lavender blooms of creeping mazus (*Mazus reptans*) pack lots of visual interest into this diminutive specimen. Tiny pebbles provide a clean backdrop that emphasizes the details of each tiny leaf.

# Kusamono Plantings

Japan's long and rich horticultural history offers up a wealth of inspiration for arrangements beyond the typical bouquet or planting. Even the most casual gardeners are familiar with the art of bonsai: the cultivation of miniature trees in containers. A classic bonsai showcases a single tree, carefully grown to remain small across decades or even centuries. Another planting style, *kusamono*, developed alongside bonsai as a showcase for a wider variety of botanical specimens. These small, potted arrangements are made up of everyday plants, from wild grasses and meadow flowers to mounds of lush moss. Originally displayed as companion pieces near a bonsai, kusamono are striking in their own right, capturing the subtle details of a particular season or natural habitat. *Kusamono* literally translates to "grass thing," indicating the humble nature of the plants found within these potted collections.

For an unexpected take on these two planting styles, try pairing a graceful sapling with a kusamono-inspired underplanting. The arrangement shown here combines the humble grasses of kusamono with the customary centerpiece of a bonsai display: a tiny, singular tree. While traditional bonsai require years of dedicated care, this arrangement uses a young sapling to achieve the same look with minimal effort. When the tree grows too large for this container, it can be moved outdoors and planted in a permanent home.

When choosing a tree for this style of planting, select one with a unique silhouette—like this asymmetrical Japanese maple with delicate, lacy leaves. Paired with a dark backdrop and a simple vessel, a shapely specimen makes a bold statement piece. (Find a guide to unusual miniature evergreens on page 319.)

# A Living Sedum Tabletop

Exceptional multitaskers for decorating and gardening projects, sedum mats were originally designed for green roofs. Incredibly hardy and dense, they also make an adaptable material for creative arrangements. Each mat is formed from a densely planted mix of sedum varieties in a lightweight coconut fiber base for water retention. This base makes it easy to cut the mats into custom shapes to fit living walls, hanging baskets, rock gardens, windowsills, and even the tabletop. Sedum can be mounted in any direction—right side up, sideways, and even upside down! Though full sun is best for thriving sedum, the mix of plants allows the mats to handle a variety of light levels; just be sure that they're never allowed to fully dry out. This striking tabletop is an arrangement best suited for special occasions—sedum should never dry completely, so after dinner it should return to a place where it can be watered.

LEFT: **FOREST GREENS** Leaving behind its usual haunts on the roof, sedum serves as a living tablecloth. (Use a disposable plastic cloth below the sedum to protect the table.)

OPPOSITE: **A FAIRY-TALE SCENE** An entire woodland garden takes root in the sedum, with creeping Jenny (*Lysimachia*), *Dichondra,* staghorn fern (*Platycerium*), *Heuchera,* and lady's slipper orchids (*Paphiopedilum*) sprouting as a centerpiece. Oversize wooden mushrooms in fanciful shapes, place mats of preserved reindeer moss in eye-popping brights, and chargers cut from live edge wood finish the forest scene.

# Floating Floral Troughs

An unconventional cross between centerpiece and installation, floating flowers take the place of a traditional tabletop arrangement for celebrations in large spaces. These dreamy displays create a sheltering canopy that fosters intimacy at each table, dotted with detailed moments to fascinate those sitting below. When hanging these weighty creations, choose a sturdy suspension system, like the steel shepherd's hooks pictured here, and a reinforced anchor in the ceiling.

**CITRUS GROVE** Drawing inspiration from the West Coast, this early-summer arrangement is woven with kumquat-studded branches. The scattered fruits add vivid color to a textural canopy of botanicals in soft hues.

**GARDENS IN THE AIR** Densely layered branches of dogwood, *Elaeagnus*, dappled willow, and ivy form a sprawling meadow in shades of green, white, cream, and apricot. Along with the kumquats, smaller focal moments are made from mingled blooms of spirea, parrot tulips, Queen Anne's lace, garden roses, and tree peonies.

# Arrangements in Lanterns

An unexpected stand-in for vases and terrariums, lanterns are a surprisingly suitable home for arrangements, particularly on a doorstep or patio table. Their decorative shapes add a structured framework to florals or small-scale plantings, while large panes of glass offer a 360-degree view of their contents. In a nod to their true function, lanterns also diffuse any lights incorporated into a display.

LEFT: **EVENING GLOW** Metal flowers entwined with foraged twigs and moss fill a row of lanterns that line a pathway for a warm welcome. These simple and enduring arrangements also fulfill a more traditional purpose, with lights concealed in the dome of each lantern offering a soft glow.

OPPOSITE: **AUTUMN BERRIES** The late-fall forest comes to life inside the wide glass panes of a simple lantern, with a mounded nest of moss supporting tiny *Sempervivum* and twigs of bittersweet vine (*Celastrus scandens*). Moss makes a natural base for arrangements in lanterns by elevating and anchoring other stems. Misted regularly, the moss and succulent base will remain fresh for an extended period, welcoming new botanicals as the seasons change.

# 5

*Seasonal Stars*

# A Year of Arrangements

The first modern greenhouses appeared in Europe during the sixteenth century, built to house tropical specimens from the era's far-reaching explorations. Farmers in the Netherlands soon saw the potential of these glass structures for cut-flower production, bringing spring blooms to life while winter winds blew outside. Modern-day arrangements benefit from this long history of year-round flower cultivation, with almost any bloom available during even the coldest days of January. But while there's no doubt that hothouse specimens can brighten a winter's day, our favorite materials remain those that celebrate the season at hand, from spring's blooming branches to autumn's colorful heirloom pumpkins.

# Arranging with Early-Spring Branches

In Japan, the word *hanami* ("flower viewing") describes the traditional celebrations of spring's short-lived flowering trees. The custom dates back over a thousand years, when plum blossoms known as *ume* attracted gatherings of admirers. Today, *sakura* (cherry blossoms) are most popular; modern-day hanami celebrations include picnics and parties, carefully planned using a blossom forecast that pinpoints peak bloom.

Brought into the home as winter turns to spring, the branches of these flowering trees—and their leafy counterparts—can be forced into early life (see page 254 to learn how). Elegant and architectural, they serve as the foundation for striking arrangements that call to mind the height of the spring garden.

Just as a traditional bouquet reveals your personal arranging style, so does your choice of branches. Their showstopping size is always impactful, while their variety of blooms, catkins, and leaves offers endless novelty. A shapely branch cut from a Japanese maple, just beginning to unfurl its trident leaves; tulip magnolia boughs draped in blush petals; the vivid, apple-green buds of an ornamental elm; a handful of willow branches dotted with catkins— all act as harbingers of the seasons to come in the world outside. Turn to pages 256–261 for a few of our favorites.

Rangy flowering quince (*Chaenomeles speciosa* 'Geisha Girl') branches with bright salmon blooms fan out atop a formal urn, paired with a base of trailing angel vine (*Muehlenbeckia complexa*) and creeping fig (*Ficus pumila*). The untamed silhouettes of the branches and vines create provocative contrast when paired with a stately urn and clean, white mantelpiece.

# Forcing Spring Branches

"Forcing" is a way to trick branches into producing early blooms or leaves, even though wintry weather persists outside. Many spring-flowering trees and shrubs form their buds in autumn; after at least two months of temperatures below 40°F, they can be forced into bloom, if given the right preparation. In most regions, branches should not be cut before January 1 in a year of typical cold, or January 15 if the weather has been especially mild.

**STEP 1:** If you're pruning anyway, select branches for forcing from among your felled limbs. If cutting specifically for forcing, look for branches with ample buds. The largest number of buds is usually found on younger branches. Flower buds are round and fat, while leaf buds are smaller and pointed.

Flower buds

Leaf buds

**STEP 2:** Carefully prune your branches on a mild day, when the temperature is above freezing. Use sharp shears or pruners to make a clean, angled cut close to a bud or side shoot, creating a branch at least a foot long. Take care to maintain the overall shape of the plant when pruning.

**STEP 3:** Bring the branches indoors and immediately place their ends in a bucket of water, misting frequently for a few days. This helps the stems and buds absorb water so they can emerge from dormancy.

**STEP 4:** After soaking, use pruning shears to remove any small twigs and buds toward the bottom 6 inches of each branch, as young shoots left underwater will rot. Trim the branches' ends once again (this is essential for water absorption). Use your shears to cut several slits at the bottom of each stem, forming a cross or star pattern.

**STEP 5:** Choose a vessel with enough weight to stay upright when filled with large branches (take into account the weight of water inside the vessel, too). A tall vessel with a narrow silhouette will keep branches upright for a shapely arrangement.

**STEP 6:** Place the branches in water and store them in a cool spot (60°F–65°F) with bright, indirect light. Replenish the water as needed, and mist the branches often until they begin to show color. This process mimics spring weather and prepares the buds to open; it may take anywhere from one to five weeks. Avoid warm areas, low humidity, and direct sunlight; these factors can prevent the branches from blooming or leafing properly.

**STEP 7:** Once the buds show color and are ready to open, create your arrangements. For best longevity, display the branches in bright, indirect light, continue to mist and change the water regularly, and add flower food with each water change. Moving the arrangement to a cool location (40°F–60°F) at night can also improve longevity. If your branches don't bloom or leaf, they may have been cut too early; you can try the same species again in a few weeks.

Vintage glass jars from Hungary hold a collection of craggy tulip magnolia branches that are just beginning to bloom. The heavy jars provide ample support for the towering branches, keeping them upright and offering space for lots of fresh water.

# Familiar Flowering & Leafing Branches

Plucked from the transitional landscape, blooming branches in unrestrained shapes create formal arrangements with a surprising twist. Familiar varieties like tulip magnolia, walnut, cherry, and maple take on new life as the centerpiece of early-spring displays.

Leafing branches can be forced just like their flowering counterparts (see page 254), yielding displays of tender greenery to invite spring indoors. Nearly any branch you like can be forced for leaves; to get the most abundant foliage, take a close look at the buds. Lots of small, pointed buds indicate that a branch will produce abundant foliage. When selecting leafy branches, look for unusual shapes and growth patterns. The season's first foliage emerges in scattered, unruly tufts on the bare black walnut branches, while the unfurling buds of Japanese maples take on a fluted, floral silhouette.

**MAGNOLIA** (*Magnolia* spp.)

**SAND CHERRY** (*Prunus pumila*)

**JAPANESE MAPLE** (*Acer palmatum*)

**EASTERN BLACK WALNUT** (*Juglans nigra*)

# Common Flowering Branches by Month

| Branch | Time to Force | Description |
|---|---|---|
| **JANUARY** | | |
| Cornelian cherry (*Cornus mas*) | 2 weeks | Yellow flowers |
| Forsythia (*Forsythia × intermedia*) | 1 to 3 weeks | Yellow flowers |
| Poplar (*Populus*) | 2 weeks | Soft, drooping catkins |
| Willow (*Salix*) | 2 weeks | Catkins |
| Witch hazel (*Hamamelis mollis*) | 1 week | Yellow flowers |
| **FEBRUARY** | | |
| Alder (*Alnus*) | 1 to 3 weeks | Catkins |
| Cherry (*Prunus*) | 2 to 4 weeks | White and pink flowers |
| Pussy willow (*Salix discolor*) | 1 to 2 weeks | Well-known fuzzy catkins |
| Quince (*Chaenomeles speciosa*) | 4 weeks | Red to orange flowers |
| Red maple (*Acer rubrum*) | 2 weeks | Red to pink flowers, followed by leaves |
| Rhododendron and azalea | 4 to 6 weeks | Many colors, later in the month |
| Silver birch (*Betula pendula*) | 2 to 4 weeks | Long-lasting catkins |
| **MARCH** | | |
| Apple (*Malus*) and crab apple (*Malus sylvestris*) | 2 to 4 weeks | White, pink, or red flowers |
| Hawthorn (*Crataegus*) | 4 to 5 weeks | White, pink, or red flowers |
| Honeysuckle (*Lonicera*) | 2 to 3 weeks | White to pink flowers |
| Lilac (*Syringa vulgaris*) | 4 to 5 weeks | Many colors |
| Mock orange (*Philadelphus coronarius*) | 4 to 5 weeks | White flowers |
| Oak (*Quercus*) | 2 to 3 weeks | Catkins |
| *Spirea* | 4 weeks | White flowers |

**WITCH HAZEL** (*Hamamelis vernalis* 'Amethyst'): A fresh take on a familiar flowering branch, this witch hazel produces reddish-purple flowers. It's equally striking in autumn, when the leaves put on a show in fiery orange and red.

# *Unusual Flowering Branches*

Beyond the familiar blossoms (see page 256), countless trees offer up their vibrant flowers as spring begins. Look to uncommon species for unique silhouettes, like the bell-shaped blossoms of enkianthus or the graceful, draping boughs of weeping cherry, every inch studded with pale pink flowers. These unexpected details inspire creative arrangements all season long and showcase the endless variation of the natural world.

**MEDITERRANEAN REDBUD**
(*Cercis siliquastrum*)

**REDVEIN ENKIANTHUS**
(*Enkianthus campanulatus*)

**ORIENTAL SPICEBUSH**
(*Lindera angustifolia*)

**WITCH ALDER** (*Fothergilla gardenii*)

**WEEPING HIGAN CHERRY**
(*Prunus pendula* 'Pendula Rosea')

**STAR MAGNOLIA** (*Magnolia stellata*)

# Unusual Leaves & Catkins

Though flowering branches may offer the showiest stems, other trees and shrubs provide unexpected interest for winter forcing in the form of unique leaves and catkins. Look for less familiar trees, like the dappled willow or yellow Japanese maple, for leaves in remarkably bright spring shades.

For more unique textures and silhouettes, consider the catkin. Instead of traditional blooms, some trees produce these clustered spikes of flowers, which form without petals for a distinctive, fuzzy texture. In fact, the term "catkin" is derived from *katteken*—a diminutive, Old Dutch word for cat—since the blooms so strongly resemble a kitten's tail. The most familiar catkin is the downy, gray oval of the pussy willow, but these unusual specimens take many shapes.

**SNAKEBARK MAPLE**
(*Acer pensylvanicum*)

**BLACK PUSSY WILLOW**
(*Salix gracilistyla* 'Melanostachys')

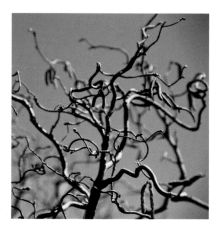

**EUROPEAN FILBERT**
(*Corylus avellana* 'Contorta')

**DAPPLED WILLOW**
(*Salix integra* 'Hakuro-nishiki')

**YELLOW JAPANESE MAPLE**
(*Acer palmatum*)

**EARLY STACHYURUS** (*Stachyurus praecox*)

**SAWTOOTH OAK** (*Quercus acutissima*): This oak produces yellow-green catkins, but its foliage is the star for winter forcing. As its name suggests, the glossy leaves are edged with angular teeth.

# Arranging with Spring Bulbs

Like forced branches, spring-blooming bulbs serve as a harbinger for the garden's return to life. These fresh-faced specimens emerge when most of the garden is still asleep. Though fleeting, their ample color celebrates a season of growth. Cut bouquets showcase bulbs' bright flowers, while planted vessels spotlight their paper bases and vivid foliage. The best bulb arrangements bring a slice of the early-spring landscape indoors through monoculture plantings, inviting a new season home with impactful collections of freshly sprouted flowers.

Growing your own bulbs requires lots of planning; many spring-flowering varieties must be planted in fall and chilled in the soil over the winter. For easier arrangements, most nurseries stock bulbs that have already sprouted around Easter. When choosing from the nursery, look for smaller plants that are just emerging; this will give spring arrangements more longevity.

Support structures are essential for bulb arrangements, because the stems become top heavy when in full bloom. Here, a bumper crop of grape hyacinths rests in a nest of budded tulip magnolia branches. Individual twigs can also be used as natural stakes for larger blooms like tulips and irises.

## Spring-Flowering Bulbs

When arranged indoors, spring bulbs—like the standout varieties below—can be temperamental and short lived. To prolong their freshness, mimic the weather of early spring by providing them with a cool, dry home away from direct sunlight.

*Muscari* 'Venus': An unusual take on the traditional grape hyacinth, muscari 'Venus' features pure white flower spikes.

**Snake's head fritillaria (*Fritillaria meleagris*)**: Named for the shape of its nodding flowers, speckled petals make fritillaria excellent for introducing pattern to an arrangement.

*Leucojum:* One of spring's earliest bloomers, this bulb produces spiky, dark green foliage topped with creamy, bell-shaped flowers.

*Narcissus* 'Tête-à-Tête': This bright yellow bloom is a favorite miniature daffodil, capturing the classic look of spring.

*Narcissus* 'Apricot Whirl': A less traditional option for daffodil lovers, this giant bloom features ruffled petals swirled with salmon and white.

**Tulip 'Black Parrot'**: The saturated burgundy of this ruffled tulip stands out against spring's pastel blooms.

**Tulip 'Lady Jane'**: With flowers striped in white and red, this unusual tulip offers a long bloom time and a spiky silhouette.

*Allium* 'Mount Everest': This fragrant and winter-hardy, late-spring bloomer can reach more than 3 feet tall, with large, round heads of tiny white flowers.

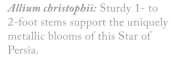

*Allium christophii:* Sturdy 1- to 2-foot stems support the uniquely metallic blooms of this Star of Persia.

*Chionodoxa* 'Blue Giant': An early-spring bloomer, this star-shaped flower produces an ombré effect as it fades from light blue to white.

# Arranging with Late-Summer Wildflowers

In late summer, wildflowers reach their highest heights and most riotous shapes, inspiring bold, large-scale arrangements that invite closer study. A rustic meadow bouquet of fresh wildflowers makes an of-the-moment adornment for the summer home, but these natural beauties are also easy to preserve for enjoyment year-round.

Wild grapevines, cattails and marsh irises, vining honeysuckle, red and yellow woodland columbine, native grasses, wild phlox and sweet William, Queen Anne's lace, bishop's weed, wild sweet pea—these are just some of the options available to the intrepid summer forager.

This simple seasonal centerpiece celebrates the bounty of late summer. Foraged wildflowers fill a weathered zinc trough with tall, wispy silhouettes that mimic the natural shapes of a summer meadow. Bold sprays of bronze sedge and fountain grasses balance the lacy blooms of Queen Anne's lace and yellow clover, while mullein seedpods add upright texture. The trough also includes white aster, achillea, peppergrass, joe-pye weed, and purple clover for an intriguing mix of textures.

# *Drying the Late-Summer Garden*

On a dry day when summer's meadows and gardens reach their peak,
plan ahead by gathering fresh stems to dry for the sparse seasons to come.
Harvested and carefully preserved as autumn approaches, dried flowers
and foliage can be incorporated into arrangements, wreaths, garlands, and
countless other projects throughout the year.

Gradually dry fresh stems by hanging them in upside-down bunches that become
eye-catching displays of their own. The late-summer stems pictured here are ideal for
drying. From left to right: palmetto; celosia; amaranthus; grasses and branches including
sea oats, yellow cigar millet, black sorghum, huckleberry, Olympia seed pods, birch
branches, curly willow, switchgrass, and miscanthus; individual hydrangea flowers;
allium seed heads.

# Arranging & Decorating with Autumn Pumpkins

One of the earliest domesticated vegetables, gourds have been cultivated for around ten thousand years. Since that time, cultures across the globe have used them for decorative and practical purposes. The tradition of carved jack-o'-lanterns came to America from Ireland, where turnips were originally carved on All Hallows' Eve. For a look that's more stylish than spooky, pumpkins also offer myriad colors, textures, shapes, and sizes for fall displays. From a tabletop bowl of tiny 'Baby Boos' to towering stacks of 'Rouge Vif d'Etampe's framing the doorway, these fall favorites make for a lighthearted season of arrangements.

Pure white pumpkins anchor a fall centerpiece inside a copper tray, providing neutral contrast for saturated autumn hues. Dried bottleneck gourds form the base of the arrangement, while strands of berry-studded bittersweet vine, ornamental cabbage, and plumes of amaranth echo the colors of fall foliage. Surrounding a pumpkin, a wreath of fresh-cut ornamental oregano completes the display.

# Pumpkins, Squash & Gourds

Fall is the perfect time to celebrate the wide variety of heirloom pumpkins.

**'Porcelain Doll':** A sensational shade of pale pink, this pumpkin has a blocky, deeply ribbed shape. Weighing in at 16 to 24 pounds, it opens to reveal deep orange flesh that's great for cooking and baking.

**'Speckled Hound':** This hybrid variety makes a graphic statement with a salmon shell splashed in chalky blue and deep green. Its fruits are slightly flattened with shallow ribbing, while the flesh inside is sweet and nutty.

**'Black Futsu':** This petite Japanese squash undergoes a colorful transformation as autumn progresses. Its bumpy rind starts out a near-black green, develops to a matte gray with touches of yellow, and finally becomes a tawny orange.

**'Flat White Boer':** With a flat silhouette that's perfect for stacking, this pure white pumpkin is a ghostly addition to the fall doorstep. This heirloom variety is native to South Africa, and is named for the country's Dutch Boer settlers.

**'Triamble':** Also known as the Shamrock, this hard-to-find pumpkin hails from Australia. Its name is derived from its unique shape, made up of three distinctive, triangular lobes.

**'Jarrahdale':** An heirloom from New Zealand, this sturdy pumpkin is a great option for fall decorating. A slate-gray rind reveals aromatic golden flesh with a mild flavor.

**'Thai Rai Kaw Tok':** A market variety that's newly arrived from Thailand, this deeply ribbed squash is speckled in shades of dark green and ivory. An exceptionally sturdy rind makes it ideal for long-term display.

**'Marina di Chioggia':** This warty, deep green pumpkin is named for the Italian fishing village of Chioggia, where it's a culinary staple. Originally from South America, it was introduced in the seventeenth century by explorers returning from the New World.

**'Red Warty Thing':** An heirloom from the late nineteenth century, this vivid, red-orange squash gets its comical name from its eye-catchingly textured skin. Weighing up to 20 pounds, it has a hard, thick rind for long-lasting display.

**'Snake Gourd':** Named for its slim, elongated shape, this squash is native to tropical regions of Southeast Asia. Its prolific vines produce an abundance of dark green fruits, which can reach several feet in length.

# *Planted Pumpkins*

Bring an autumn garden to the table with these pumpkin "planters." Tiny variegated specimens topped with single succulents make a sweet gift for each place setting, while taller trios edged in moss and foraged finds serve as a colorful centerpiece.

**What You'll Need:**
- Miniature pumpkins
- Pumpkin carving knife and scoop
- Small succulents
- Paraffin wax
- Hot plate
- Spoon
- Potting soil
- Moss

**STEP 1:** Carve a hole into the top of a pumpkin that is large enough to fit the plant you've selected.

**STEP 2:** Once the top is removed, carefully hollow out the inside of the pumpkin. To ensure that the pumpkin stays fresh, scrape down the flesh as thoroughly as possible.

**STEP 3:** Melt the paraffin wax over the hot plate, then spoon the wax into the hollow pumpkin. Swirl the wax around to make sure the interior and lip are completely coated, then set the pumpkin aside until the wax is cool and dry.

**STEP 4:** Fill the sealed pumpkin with potting soil and place a plant inside. Fill out the edges of the planting with moss as needed.

# Decoupaged Pumpkins

A unique way to combine pumpkins with fall's lingering foliage, these botanical beauties are a simple alternative to the jack-o'-lantern—no carving tools required. This decoupaging technique allows the pumpkin to remain whole, keeping it fresh longer than a carved specimen. Dainty leaves and feathery ferns make for especially striking decoupage materials, their intricate silhouettes showing in sharp contrast against the pale, creamy rinds of heirloom pumpkin varieties (see page 267).

**What You'll Need:**
- Delicate fern fronds, leaves, and vine clippings
- Pumpkin (we used a white Casper pumpkin)
- Cloth
- Spray adhesive
- Paintbrush
- Decoupage glue

**STEP 1:** Select your stems. Light, delicate botanicals will adhere more easily to the pumpkin.

**STEP 2:** Prep your pumpkin. Using the stem as a center point, plan where you'll adhere your chosen cuttings. Use a damp cloth to wipe any dirt from the rind and dry thoroughly.

**STEP 3:** Adhere your plants. Using a spray adhesive, lightly mist the back of your botanicals. Moving quickly, tack the plants to the surface of the pumpkin. Keeping the leaves flush against the rind, use a paintbrush to spread a thin layer of decoupage glue over the surface of each leaf, pressing down any sections that pop up. Allow the decoupage glue to dry, then repeat with three to four additional layers, until all the plants have been adhered.

**STEP 4:** Working in a sunny location will help speed the drying process and allow the botanicals to adhere more quickly to the rind. Once the clippings are secure, however, the pumpkin should be moved to a dry, shady location to fully set overnight.

ABOVE: Try arranging several fern fronds to create a starry pattern that radiates outward from the stem.

OPPOSITE: Once the decoupaging process is complete, pair a decorated pumpkin with a natural bed of foraged vines, pinecones, and moss for a display inspired by the autumn forest.

# Spotlight on Christmas

*berries & boughs*

———

As the holidays approach, winter's long nights give rise to a season of domestic celebration. Home becomes a beacon framed in starry lights, bedecked with fresh greens, and filled with friends and family. Though blanketed in frost, the garden offers up its finest ornaments in the bountiful forms of vibrant winterberry, merry mistletoe, and, of course, fresh and fragrant greens.

These spirited adornments from the natural world set the scene for a holiday that celebrates tradition and the closing of the year. We join with friends around the crackling flames of the fire pit and before the twinkling boughs of the Christmas tree. In these simple moments, we gather as the year comes to an end, reflecting on our merriest memories and looking ahead with hope for the seasons to come.

## Day Trip
# Winterberry Season at Schmidt's Tree Farm

Reindeer, hot cocoa, and wagon rides . . . Schmidt's Tree Farm offers all the trappings of an enchanted Christmas-tree hunt, including three acres of cut-your-own evergreens. American favorites including the Canaan fir, Douglas fir, and Colorado blue spruce are on offer, as are Europe's top pick—the Nordmann fir—and many more. While these traditional trees may draw crowds to the farm, an unexpected holiday crop enhances its hills: brilliant red and gold winterberry.

The farm's owners, Joan and Ellis, discovered winterberry over fifteen years ago thanks to a scholarly visitor promoting the crop. As it turned out, their property in Landenberg, Pennsylvania, was a premier growing site for this holiday showstopper. This revelation tapped into Ellis's passion for growing new plants and his ongoing dedication to discovering and cultivating the species that perform best on his land.

A coveted seasonal decoration thanks to its festive color, winterberry loses its leaves in late autumn after the first hard frost, leaving dense berry bunches behind. Treasured by birds and home decorators alike, the fruit remains on its lengthy stems all season long, making a vibrant addition to wreaths, festoons, and swags—or a striking stand-alone statement.

# Yuletide in Scandinavia

During a Nordic winter, long nights and frigid temperatures make the cozy gatherings and glowing lights of Christmas all the more welcome.

Scandinavian cultures are rich in holiday tradition, celebrating the season with simple, natural décor, hearty meals, and fireside evenings. The holiday season extends far beyond Christmas Day in these northern regions, filling the month of December with warm-spirited gatherings and candlelit nights.

**ST. LUCIA'S DAY:** Observed on December 13, St. Lucia's Day marks the beginning of Christmas celebrations across Scandinavia. Feasts honoring St. Lucia, an early Christian martyr, once coincided with the winter solstice; this connection soon transformed the occasion into a festival of light. In modern times, St. Lucia's Day is observed with candlelit processions led by a young girl dressed as Lucia in a long white gown and a crown of greens and tapers. Those who join her in the procession also hold candles and sing traditional songs. During the procession and at home, traditional sweet buns called *lussekutter*—flavored with saffron, cardamom, and raisins—are enjoyed with warming coffee or mulled wine.

**JÓL LOG:** The *jól* log takes its name from a Norse word for the winter solstice, Jól (often translated as Jule or Yule), a time when a log was burned to celebrate the sun's impending return. According to tradition, early jól logs were entire trees, pulled from the forest by a team of horses. The largest end of the tree was placed in the hearth, then slowly fed into the fire during the twelve days of Christmas, filling the home with good fortune as it burned. Though the size of the log has diminished in modern times, this ritual remains at the heart of Scandinavian Christmas. Jól logs should still be impressive in size, for a lasting burn that may take place indoors or out. Burned under the stars or in the fireplace, they create a sociable scene for toasting, mulling, feasting, and ushering in the new year.

**GLÖGG:** A festive libation for holiday revelry, *glögg* (pronounced glug) is a Scandinavian take on mulled wine. Warm and fragrant, this holiday brew starts with red wine, which is then mixed with classic mulling spices like cinnamon, cardamom, and cloves. For a Nordic twist, add a hearty splash of aquavit, a spirit distilled with savory spices like caraway or dill.

**WHITE LIGHTS:** In Sweden, winter is dominated by two hues: the black of a nearly twenty-four-hour night and the white of fallen snow. These steadfast shades paint defining lines across the landscape, which is lit during the holidays by seas of flickering white lights. Refracting off ice and glass, they produce a magical glow. This enchanting custom dates to the 1800s, when Swedish families would place a single candle in their windows on Christmas Eve, allowing it to burn for twenty-four hours as a salutation to passers-by. Soon the convention extended to offices, cafés, and shops throughout the entire month of December, and spread through Scandinavia to create today's twinkling tableaux.

# A Natural Holiday

In the harsh winters of colonial America, immigrants from England, Scotland, Ireland, Holland, and Germany yearned for the familiar holiday traditions of their homelands. They turned to the most abundant resource of their new country—its boundless wilderness—to craft seasonal décor. Using the wealth of natural materials around them, they celebrated a simple Christmas with wild, foraged decorations—sprays of bright red winterberry, glossy holly branches, and simple, fragrant evergreen boughs, made all the more beautiful in the golden glimmer of candlelight.

Our Christmas décor hearkens back to these early traditions, as we adopt a natural perspective on transforming the holiday home. Illuminated structures and evergreen wreaths deck our pathways and doorsteps, while bright, blooming bulbs, fresh greens, and glowing candles bring joy to indoor spaces. At the heart of the home, fresh and festive trees serve as the centerpiece of the season, whether wild and unadorned or fully decorated with heirloom ornaments and twinkling lights. These simple adornments anchor a quiet, honest season of celebration that forgoes the trends of the moment. Best of all, they invite us in from the frozen world outside, to gather with those we hold dearest and find deeper meaning in a natural Christmas.

PREVIOUS PAGES: Use botanical accents to emphasize permanent architectural elements of your home. Draw attention to a colorful door with a contrasting wreath, accent a roofline with a thick garland of evergreen boughs, or tuck a bundle of branches into an all-season planter.

OPPOSITE: Stately noble firs stand tall in the tree lot, waiting to take their places in holiday homes. These noteworthy trees, with a wonderfully airy and open growth pattern, are among our favorite evergreens.

# 1

*Greet Them with Greens*

# Our Holiday Philosophy

Shaped by generations of tradition, holiday celebrations take many forms. In Scandinavia, the holiday season is defined by light, the long nights of a Nordic winter inspiring cozy, candlelit gatherings accented with simple botanical décor. In Germany, bustling Christmas markets spring up in the streets, filled with seasonal treats, fresh greens, mulled wine, and merry revelers. In the United States, the selection of the tree often marks the official start of the holiday season, serving as the centerpiece for December's festivities. Varied as they are, common threads connect these traditions: a desire to join with friends and family and an eagerness to invite the winter world into our homes through naturally festive décor.

The following pages offer our philosophy for gathering and decorating during the Christmas season, along with our favorite natural materials for creating a beautiful holiday home, indoors and out.

# Create Gathering Spaces

At the heart of the holiday season is the desire to connect with loved ones from near and far over shared memories and hopes for the year ahead. When decorating for the season, look for opportunities to create places to gather throughout the home. Make a crackling hearth the focal point of the living room with the addition of fresh greens, encourage guests to linger at the table with a candlelit centerpiece, and dress the tree in heirloom ornaments that spark merry reminiscences of holidays past.

Though temperatures drop as Christmas approaches, don't overlook the possibilities of outdoor spaces for seasonal get-togethers. Illuminate the landscape with lighted structures (see page 298) to encourage twilight strolls in the snow, or create an unexpected space for winter gatherings by designing an outdoor room with a crackling fire pit as a centerpiece.

Paired with cozy throws, warming drinks, and impromptu seating, the fire pit becomes an invitation to enjoy the snowy world outside. Here, a decorative wood stack frames the fire pit to create a defined and welcoming space.

# Decorate with
# Natural Materials

When early December arrives, take up a firewood carrier or an oversize basket and set off on a foraging excursion; the time has arrived to gather fresh, natural materials for handcrafted holiday decorations. With just a little searching, the quiet winter landscape reveals a wealth of decorative possibilities, from fragrant evergreen boughs and spiny pinecones to berry-laden bushes, spongy moss, and knotty twigs. Winter weather proves too harsh for many plants, but these hardy specimens can be used to create long-lasting décor indoors and out, even as snow blankets the landscape.

Far from pristine, these organic elements' imperfect edges and weathered stems reflect nature's cycles of growth and decay. Their fresh scents and saturated shades, however, offer a more hopeful message for midwinter: the natural world endures through these short, dark days and will soon spring to life once again, bountiful and bright.

The following pages showcase four of our favorite natural palettes for winter decorating, made up of fresh, foraged finds and dried botanicals saved from seasons past. Designed to offer rich, complementary shades, these natural collections can be shaped into wreaths and garlands, tucked among the boughs of the tree, showcased in planters that have been emptied at the end of the growing season, or used in countless other outdoor spaces.

A fresh marketplace showcases the abundance of color and texture offered by winter's branches and stems, from the leathery, two-tone leaves of magnolia to the tiny, silver pods of eucalyptus.

# Four Natural Winter Palettes

## *Christmas Classic*

A merry mix of fresh greens, bright branches, and festive berries

**CURLY PINE**

**MING PINE**

**MAGNOLIA**

**INCENSE CEDAR**

**RED WINTERBERRY**

**RED TWIG DOGWOOD**

**ROSE HIPS**

**SILVER BRUNIA**

## *Midwinter Fire*

Saturated reds, sunset oranges, and petal pinks unite for fireside hues

**HEATHER**

**PLUM BRUNIA**

**GOMPHRENA**

**MIXED BRUNIA**

**BANKSIA**

**PLUMOSUM**

**CELOSIA**

**ORANGE WINTERBERRY**

# Blue Sage

A refreshing collection of flowers and foliage in pale mint and dusty blue

**PRIVET BERRY**

**SILVER DOLLAR EUCALYPTUS**

**SILVER TREE LEUCADENDRON**

**SILVER BRUNIA**

**SNOWY EVERGREEN**

**KOCHIA**

**BLUE HYDRANGEA**

**EUCALYPTUS PODS**

# Golden Wheat

Shades of mustard and golden brown combine for a warm welcome

**SEEDED EUCALYPTUS**

**GRAPEVINE**

**GOLDEN SEEDED EUCALYPTUS**

**IMMORTELLE**

**STEMMED ARTICHOKE**

**POPPY PODS**

**ALLIUM SEED HEAD**

**BANKSIA**

# 2

*Winter Wonders*

# Outdoor Décor
# for a Spirited Season

Beyond the snug confines of the home, the stark winter landscape provides a clean slate for holiday decorating on a grand scale. Stately garden structures transform into dramatic installations, flanking the drive and doorstep with dazzling lights. Fresh wreaths frame a welcoming entryway. And Christmas trees find unexpected outdoor applications to spread good cheer beyond the home. Our exploration of exterior décor begins with ideas to greet guests as they approach the home, followed by welcoming designs to deck out the doorstep. Finally, we'll share our favorite ways to decorate barns and outbuildings in grand style.

# Lights from Pathway to Porch

Scattered across the lawn and garden, unexpected moments of illumination extend holiday décor well beyond the home, and serve as the first sign of welcome for arriving guests. Bright outdoor displays also provide a counterpoint to the early darkness of winter evenings, inviting us to linger outside on even the coldest nights.

Rather than lighting the entire home or yard, focus on a few high-impact displays that frame the entrance and approach. Take advantage of permanent garden installations, such as containers and metal structures, from which warm-weather plantings have been removed. These large-scale fixtures offer a ready-made framework for strands of glowing lights.

To outline a structure in lights, use metal cable ties, which can be found at most hardware stores. Trim each tie with metal snips to fit around the frame of the structure, then use the bands to secure the light cord. The key is keeping the strand flat and taut so the bulbs stay upright; try placing a cable tie close to the base of each bulb, plus additional ties between bulbs.

LEFT: **A STARRY SPHERE** Illuminated using the method described above, a spherical structure rests in a nest of fresh evergreen boughs and oversize metal leaves atop a frost-proof planter.

OPPOSITE: **THE WELCOMING COMMITTEE** Spheres of lights and vines perched atop all-weather pots line the driveway for a warm introduction to the holiday home.

# The Woodland Doorstep

The home's quintessential welcoming space during any season, the doorstep takes on special significance during the holidays. As the place where we greet our Christmas visitors, the doorstep should provide ample cheer and a warm invitation into the home. Fresh trees provide a long-lasting and unexpected option for doorstep décor, offering lots of natural color, texture, and detail. While choosing your tree for inside the home, select a few more firs to create a grove flanking the door. This forest in miniature makes a major statement, immersing guests in greenery and lights as soon as they arrive.

**MIRRORED ELEMENTS** Fiberstone planters hold twin silvertip firs that flank the entryway, uplit to accentuate their spartan shapes. The planters provide an easy solution for concealing a stand, a water reservoir for the tree, or any extra light cords. An oversize garland extends beyond the door frame in a welcoming gesture to finish the look.

**A FOREST AT HOME** Play with scale by mixing full-size trees with tabletop firs and evergreen topiaries. Place the largest trees as a backdrop, then add smaller trees atop plant stands, with the topiaries in planters below for a final layer of green. An oversize wreath forms the centerpiece for this woodland welcome.

In lieu of a traditional bow, accent a classic evergreen wreath with an effortlessly knotted length of ribbon, left long and trailing for subtle movement.

# European Wintergreen Wreaths

European-style evergreen wreaths conceal the secret to long-lasting freshness at their center: a moisture-retaining hay base ensures that they'll stay lush all season long. Their simple, full shape makes a stand-alone statement or welcomes foraged accents like berries, twigs, cones, and even tiny bulbs.

**What You'll Need:**
- Hay wreath form
- Garden snips
- Fresh evergreen branches
- Green floral wire
- Wire snips
- Berries, cones, and other foraged accents (optional)
- Vessel for soaking the wreath

**STEP 1:** Cut enough sturdy greens to cover the entire hay form; each piece should be several inches long. Select a sturdy evergreen like spruce as a base, plus others, such as cedar and boxwood, for layering.

**STEP 2:** Bend the cuttings to match the shape of the hay form, then wrap them with wire to secure to the base. (Leave the wire on its spool and use one continuous strand for wrapping.)

**STEP 3:** Continue to cover the hay form with greens, adding layers and using smaller sprigs to fill any gaps until no hay is showing. Pull the wire tight as you work to make the circle even and corral any stray tips.

**STEP 4:** Layer on the other varieties of greens, using the same wire-wrapping method to maintain a tight, dense form.

**STEP 5:** Once the greenery is complete, use floral wire to attach accents as desired.

**STEP 6:** Submerge the completed wreath in a bath of water, taking care to thoroughly soak the hay form at the center. This reservoir of water will extend the life of the wreath, particularly if it's sheltered from rain or snow.

# Decorating with Wreaths

Framed by a frosty window or decking the entryway, inventive wreath displays send the season's greetings to both visiting friends and passers-by.

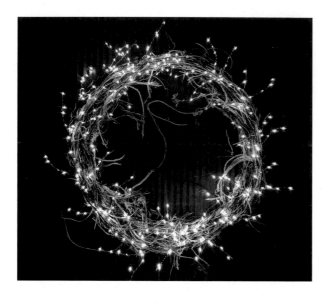

TOP: **LIGHTS & VINES** Dress up a simple wreath of dried honeysuckle or grapevine with densely wrapped strands of extra-fine lights. Let the ends of the light strands trail outward to mirror the natural shape of the vines.

ABOVE: **SUSPENDED STYLE** Replace a traditional wreath hanger with wide burlap ribbon to accent a shaggy circle of greens.

RIGHT: **BUILD A STACK** Instead of packing away your frost-resistant planters (see page 40) during the winter months, top them with stacks of wreaths to create impromptu topiaries on the doorstep. Alternate evergreen rings with looser wreaths of wild vine for defined, contrasting layers.

**RIBBONS & BELLS** For a friendly wreath topper, swap long, informal tails of wide ribbon for traditional multilooped bows and add a leather strap of sleigh bells that mimics the ribbon's silhouette and that will chime in greeting when the door opens. An age-old symbol of holiday cheer, these merry bells once served a practical purpose: sleighs moved silently over winter snow and couldn't stop quickly, so the jingle of bells warned other travelers of their approach.

# Bright Branches
# for Winter Planters

Found and foraged branches provide ample interest for winter containers, emptied of their fair-weather plantings. Leave planters in place on the patio, in the garden, or at the door, and simply refill them with these natural adornments for a welcoming burst of color that will last through the holidays. A caution for repurposing planters: be sure to choose vessels made from frost-resistant materials to avoid cracking if water caught inside freezes and thaws (see page 40 for frost ratings of many common container materials).

**OVERSIZE ELEMENTS** Large branches—like fiery red twig dogwood (*Cornus alba* 'Sibirica')—can be placed upright in containers for exceptionally dramatic structures. Clusters of red winterberry carry color through the base of this cube planter, lined with a layer of black mondo grass left over from autumn.

**BOLD BRANCHES** Substantial birch logs serve as the centerpiece for this abundant nest of favorite winter branches, including red twig dogwood, winterberry, Douglas fir, boxwood, and a mix of standard and willow leaf eucalyptus. When choosing foliage branches for outdoor use, keep durability in mind; eucalyptus offers lots of texture while standing up to the elements.

**THE MERRY DOORSTEP** After nightfall, use lights to emphasize the fiery colors of winter branches. Anchor a dense cluster of branches in the leftover soil of a weatherproof planter, then nestle lights at the base of the branches to create a dramatic, glowing display that frames the entryway.

# An Expansive Evergreen Wreath

Windowless walls on barns or outbuildings provide a blank canvas that welcomes wreaths of remarkable size. These large-scale creations offer the opportunity to showcase winter's surprising botanical abundance. When crafting a colossal wreath, consider the sight lines of its location; these impressive installations are especially impactful when spotted from afar. Also be sure to balance dramatic scale with small, thoughtful details. The substantial wreath opposite fills an entire wall with elaborate layers of winter branches and berries, each offering unique textures and colors to invite closer observation. A wall of weathered barn wood makes the perfect backdrop for this striking installation.

## What You'll Need:
- Large grapevine wreath base
- Hanging brackets (optional)
- Large screws
- Foraged bare branches
- Mixed evergreen boughs
- Floral wire
- Wire snips
- Incense cedar branches
- Red dogwood twigs
- Red winterberry stems

**STEP 1:** Choose your grapevine wreath base. It should be large enough to let some of the bigger branches extend beyond the edge of the wall, and sturdy enough to support all the branches and greens. Anchor the grapevine wreath to the wall as a base using sturdy brackets or screws.

**STEP 2:** Arrange a few large, bare branches so they radiate outward from the vine base. Affix each branch to the wall with screws, giving the appearance of growth from the central wreath.

**STEP 3:** Add a layer of mixed evergreen boughs. Tuck the branches into the perimeter of the grapevine base, pointing outward to blend in with the foraged branches. Use floral wire to anchor the boughs as needed.

**STEP 4:** Use additional layers of evergreens and incense cedar to fill out the center of the wreath, then accentuate the design with spikes of red dogwood and clusters of red winterberry. Use floral wire as needed to attach the cutting securely.

# A Forest Fireplace

An outdoor mantelpiece topped with a grove of tiny trees brings
unexpected whimsy to an otherwise barren exterior wall during
the winter months. A vintage mantelpiece forms the foundation
of this look; try scouting the offerings at an architectural salvage
company for unusual antique options.

To create this festive outdoor scene, start by locating a
blank wall and affixing a mantel of your choice. Choose small-
scale evergreens or cut the tops from larger trees to create your
miniature forest, anchoring each one to the wall. To keep the
trees flush against the building, cut away a few branches at the
back if needed, and finish with a matching evergreen wreath.

This holiday vignette is especially striking in regions with ample snowfall;
the branches and mantelpiece become even more beautiful beneath a
blanket of white.

# 3

*Hearth & Home*

## Welcoming Christmas Indoors

Make merry around the house by scattering small, festive moments of naturally inspired décor in every corner. Drape the hearth in foraged garlands, hang rich wreaths of gilded botanicals, top the table with fresh greens, and layer every space with lights that warm even the frostiest nights. This exploration of indoor décor considers the many spaces where friends and family gather to celebrate the season, including inventive ideas for a merry mantel, a festive tabletop, and unexpected places to display trees of every size.

# Collected Circles

The tradition of wreaths at the doorstep was established in the sixteenth century and remains a hallmark of modern holiday décor. Carry fresh outdoor greens to indoor spaces with wreaths displayed in the entryway, foyer, or mudroom. In place of a single statement wreath, consider a collection of slender circlets. Their simple silhouettes form repeating patterns, with an impact that exceeds their diminutive scale.

ABOVE: **MANY MAKE ONE** Multipaned windows create tiny frames to showcase a collection of simple boxwood or evergreen circlets, suspended with bright ribbons reminiscent of holiday packages.

OPPOSITE: **A GREEN TRIO** In place of a single statement wreath, accent the door with a graduated trio of smaller circlets, joined together with loops of ribbon.

**A MERRY MANTEL** A large-scale wreath of weathered metal leaves and flowers sets the tone for an elegant, metallic-accented mantelpiece, anchored by a trio of cloches. Scattered points of light carry the glow of the fire upward, and introduce a subtle shimmer with the help of burnished elements.

# Curiosities under Glass

In nineteenth-century France, newly married couples preserved mementos from their wedding day inside a glass cloche, creating a display known as a *globe de mariée*. Over the years, they would add more tokens—locks of their children's hair, photographs, jewelry, and symbolic golden charms—until the cloche became a miniature reflection of their lives together. Today, this tradition adapts beautifully to holiday displays under glass; ornate collections of preserved botanicals, touched with gilded accents, make for an elegant way to dress the mantel. The subtle metallic tones of these everlasting creations catch the light of the crackling fire below to create a warm and welcoming scene.

**A GILDED COLLECTION** For a nod to the traditional *globe de mariée*, mix metal flowers and foliage with natural, dried specimens that have been painted gold to create a glittering bouquet. For more on gilding, see page 320.

**FOREST FINDS** Mingle foraged elements—like a craggy branch—with polished glass pieces to create a display with playful contrast.

# A Tiny Tree

For an enduring touch of holiday green, consider a tiny planted conifer rather than a cut juletrae (as seen on page 326). The saplings of species with unusual colors, textures, and silhouettes bring the forest indoors for a wonderfully natural Christmas. Best of all, young trees can be planted outside after the holidays, where they'll grow to full size in the years to come, serving as a reminder of celebrations past.

ABOVE: **GREEN GIFTS** Miniature evergreens make a surprising gift for the holiday hostess, tucked inside a glass hurricane and wrapped in lights.

LEFT: **ROOT AND BRANCH** For natural cheer, root an evergreen cutting (see page 230 for more on rooting) in a glass bauble vase, paired with a matching cloche.

## Miniature Evergreens

These evergreen species offer sculptural saplings with a remarkable array of growth habits, from sleek and slender to graceful and drooping.

**Japanese cedar (*Cryptomeria japonica* 'Black Dragon').** This slow-growing dwarf conifer is prized by gardeners for its remarkable foliage, which matures from bright green to nearly black.

**Blue atlas cedar (*Cedrus atlantica*):** Like its weeping cousin, this cedar is noteworthy for its striking blue hue. Its young, slender limbs will spread into a majestic, pyramidal form as it grows.

**Deodar cedar (*Cedrus deodara*):** The Deodar cedar, native to the Himalayas, features gently drooping branches with gray-green needles. *Deodar* is derived from the Sanskrit name for the species, *devadaru*, which means "timber of the gods."

**Japanese white pine (*Pinus parviflora*):** This graceful pine is native to steep slopes and ridges in Japan and Korea. Its finely textured needles are long and brushy, with a blue-green hue.

**Weeping blue atlas cedar (*Cedrus atlantica* 'Glauca Pendula'):** Native to the Atlas Mountains of Algeria and Morocco, this cedar is descriptively named for its drooping habit and unusual, powder blue shade.

**White spruce (*Picea glauca*):** An upright shape and stiff, blue-green needles make this medium-size conifer the perfect choice for a classic Christmas look.

# A Touch of Gold

In the Shakespearean idiom, "gilding the lily" indicated the unnecessary adornment of an already-beautiful object. During the holidays, however, a golden touch is always welcome. Two simple techniques can be used to transform fresh or dried stems into shimmering ornaments for the season. The first uses gilding paste, a pigmented wax that comes in a variety of metallic finishes; it produces an overall sheen and is best suited to sturdy, smooth specimens like magnolia leaves. The second uses gold or silver spray paint to create a marbled, metallic effect on fresh botanicals. (See how both techniques are used to decorate a garden-inspired Christmas tree on page 338.)

## GILDING PASTE TECHNIQUE

**What You'll Need:**
- Sturdy, smooth botanicals (fresh, dried, or preserved)
- Soft paintbrush
- Gilding paste
- Soft cloth or paint sponge, plus a soft cloth for finishing

**STEP 1:** Select your botanicals and clean the surface with a soft paintbrush to remove any dirt or debris.

**STEP 2:** Dip the cloth or sponge into the gilding paste and apply a light coat to the surface of the botanicals. Apply thinly for a subtle sheen, or use a thicker layer for a bolder metallic finish.

**STEP 3:** Let dry for 12 hours, then gently buff with a clean, dry cloth to produce the gilded finish.

## SPRAY PAINT TECHNIQUE

**What You'll Need:**
- Large bucket
- Fresh botanicals
- Metallic spray paint
- Newspaper

**STEP 1:** Fill the bucket partially with water, then spray the metallic paint onto the surface of the water to form a thin, swirling layer.

**STEP 2:** Dunk the fresh botanicals through the paint into the water, then draw them out carefully so the paint adheres to random portions of each stem.

**STEP 3:** Place the botanicals on layers of newspaper and let dry fully.

Eucalyptus cuttings treated with gilding paste accent a circlet wreath of faux golden snowdrops and fresh evergreen sprigs.

# The Holiday Glow

The languid flickering of candlelight recalls a slower time, when our daily rhythms were ruled by sunrise and sunset. Winter's short windows of daylight once set an unhurried pace for the season, with candlelight inviting friends and family to gather after the day's work was done. In today's holiday home, flickering candles—and string lights that mimic their golden glow—continue to inspire a convivial atmosphere, welcoming us indoors on a winter's night.

**BRIGHT BAUBLES** Bud vases—like these circular baubles paired with petite steel plant stands for variations in height—can take the place of traditional votives for the tabletop. Tuck a tangle of string lights on slender wire inside each vase to create starry constellations.

**ILLUMINATED BOTANICALS** Gilded elements, like this botanical wreath, reflect lights for added impact. Here, a dark backdrop creates a defined silhouette for the glowing circlet.

**TALL TAPERS** Horizontal wreath centerpieces topped with taper candles draw inspiration from the Advent wreath tradition. Originating in Germany, these wreaths marked the weeks of Advent, with families counting down to Christmas by lighting a new candle on each of the four Sundays before the holiday. To transform any wreath into a candlelit centerpiece, simply add taper clips or stakes among the greens.

# Fire & Ice Branches

Splashing bold color across the stark landscape, flame willow, red twig dogwood, and winterberry are winter's most spectacular branches. Arranged in large bunches, these fiery botanicals make a dramatic accent piece for the sideboard or mantel. A bundle of branches is especially striking when showcased in a simple column vase, given an icy finish with a clever application of paraffin.

**What You'll Need:**
- Large, clear vase
- Paraffin wax
- Saucepan
- Flame willow, red twig dogwood, and/or winterberry branches
- Citrus-based natural cleaner

**STEP 1:** Fill a large vase partway with cold water and ice cubes. (Very cold water is key, as it cools the wax to protect the branches' bark layer from damage.)

**STEP 2:** Melt the paraffin wax in the saucepan until liquid. Let the paraffin cool until it's nearly ready to solidify, then gently pour a layer onto the surface of the water.

**STEP 3:** When the wax has solidified enough to support the branches, insert them upright through the wax layer and into the water.

**STEP 4:** Once the wax is fully dried, use the cleaner to remove any excess wax from the sides of the vase.

# The Jolly Juletrae

In Danish, the word for a Christmas tree of any size is *juletrae*; we find this cheerful name especially well suited to festive miniature trees, crafted by hand from evergreen cuttings gathered in the winter woods. Simple handfuls of twigs and greens can be transformed into diminutive DIY trees that spread holiday cheer to every corner of the home. Tucked into miniature planters, tiny juletraes make a charming way to top the table, sideboard, or mantel during the holidays.

## What You'll Need:
- Evergreen cuttings or tiny bare twigs
- Straight, leafless twig (to be used as a "trunk")
- Small terra-cotta pot
- Fine crushed gravel
- Floral wire and wire snips or a glue gun
- Fresh moss
- Accents like faux snow or winterberry sprigs (optional)

**STEP 1**: Gather a few handfuls of tiny pine sprigs or leafless twigs around 3 inches in length; these will serve as the "branches." You'll also need a larger twig that's straight and sturdy enough to serve as the "trunk" of the juletrae.

**STEP 2**: Choose a small pot and fill it three-quarters of the way with gravel to anchor the trunk.

**STEP 3**: Leaving a section at the base of the twig bare to serve as the trunk of the tree, begin attaching the evergreen cuttings or tiny twigs to form branches. Use floral wire or dots of hot glue to affix each one. Start with the lowest branches, pointing each sprig downward to create a tapered shape, and layer additional cuttings or twigs until you reach the top of the trunk.

**STEP 4**: If you'd like, add one or two tiny clippings facing upward to form the crown.

**STEP 5**: Anchor the finished tree in the gravel, then top the pot with fresh moss, pressing down gently to help the tree stay in place. Add a dusting of faux snow or berry sprigs atop the moss, if desired. Mist the moss regularly to extend the life of the display.

# Tabletop Trees

While most Americans prefer floor-to-ceiling firs, some European traditions
dictate that the holiday tree shouldn't exceed 4 feet in height. Small-scale
evergreens between 3 and 4 feet tall provide a glimpse of green in parts of the
home not suited to a full-size fir. These "tabletop" trees bring Christmas cheer
to transitional spaces like the porch or mudroom, as well as unexpected indoor
locations like a sideboard or staircase.

LEFT: **BAUBLES & BULBS** Mimic
the look of a full-size fir with
miniature globe ornaments
and lights that match the
scale of a tabletop tree.
In transitional spaces like
the entryway, add fresh-cut
evergreen boughs and a
dusting of faux snow to your
fully decorated tree, creating
a connection to the world
just outside the door.

OPPOSITE: **LIGHTS & GREENS**
Tabletop trees with rustic
silhouettes are particularly
well suited for understated
adornments, like a casually
wrapped strand of globe
lights and a planter plucked
from the garden in place of
a skirt.

# Floating Firs

Suspended in a high-ceilinged space, a hanging Christmas tree makes a dazzling centerpiece for the holiday home, inspiring childlike wonder in all who see it. These trees trace their roots to Eastern Europe: an upside-down spruce was once a common sight in Polish and Ukrainian homes.

The original hanging trees were decked with fruit and nuts, seasonal sweets, gilded pinecones, and paper or straw decorations; today, these lofty installations welcome snowy flocking, lots of lights, and jewel-bright ornaments. A bonus: they keep delicate decorations out of reach of curious pets and kids!

If installing a floating tree at home, be sure to hang it from a sturdy bracket that's securely anchored in the ceiling. Use a pair of cables attached near the base of the trunk to support the tree and keep it steady. (Never hang with cables near the tip—this can pull off the top of the tree.)

Since it's impossible to water a hanging tree, faux firs are best used to achieve this look. To conceal the stand, create a "root system" that makes the tree appear plucked fresh from the forest: gather and clean a bundle of gnarled roots, twigs, or vines, then attach them to the base of the trunk and stand using floral wire.

ABOVE: **WOODLAND ACCENTS** A table below the floating tree can hold the season's gifts, or be covered in moss to mimic the forest floor.

OPPOSITE: **A SNOWBOUND SCENE** A heavily flocked faux tree floats in a sea of lights to create a dreamy winter wonderland. This tree offers another option for concealing a stand: a cluster of hanging pinecones with a matching frosty finish.

# 4

*The Christmas Tree*

# Fresh & Festive Evergreens

The tradition of the Christmas tree began in Northern Europe, where it was a simple affair. Bare evergreens were first brought indoors as reminders of spring during December's dark and cold days. As the practice spread throughout Europe, creativity grew. Some households hung trees upside down, suspended from the ceiling or a chandelier. Others preferred hawthorn trees or branches, placed in pots to force holiday blooms. Where trees were scarce, pyramids of wood or even broomsticks served as stand-ins.

Though Christmas trees are holiday icons in the United States today, their stateside popularity wasn't cemented until the mid-nineteenth century, when, in 1850, *Godey's Lady's Book* published a photo of Queen Victoria's Christmas celebration—complete with a Christmas tree.

A modern Christmas mingles the past and present, balancing the tree's humble appeal with the festive flash of ornaments for a spirited season. For many, the selection of a tree marks the start of the Christmas season, whether it entails a bundled-up trek into the woods or a family visit to the local tree farm.

# Finding Your Tree

America's most popular Christmas trees include Scotch pine, Douglas fir, Fraser fir, balsam fir, and white pine. These widespread species have long been at the heart of the holiday season, but less conventional—and less manicured—varieties like the lodgepole pine and silvertip fir offer captivating textures and ample character. (See opposite for a few of our favorite varieties.) Before layering your tree with lights and ornaments this Christmas, take a moment to consider the natural beauty of its evergreen boughs.

The silvertip fir (*Abies magnifica*) brightens the holiday home with a natural shimmer that radiates from the eponymous silver-gray tips of its branches. This remarkable color pairs with a symmetrical and open growth pattern for a tree like no other, beautiful as a stand-alone statement or fully decked in ornaments and lights.

# Uncommon Christmas Trees

Celebrate the wild beauty of the winter forest with these unique, rugged evergreens.

**Canaan fir (*Abies balsamea* var. *phanerolepis*):** This unique tree—actually a variety of balsam fir—was first discovered in the highest elevations of the Appalachian Mountains. Moderately sized, the Canaan fir has dense, dark green needles with a silvery underside. Uniform branches, a pyramidal habit, and excellent needle retention make it a long-lasting choice for the holidays.

**Nordmann fir (*Abies nordmanniana*):** The Nordmann fir originated in the rugged Caucasus region of Europe and is the classic European Christmas tree. Stout and symmetrical, it's densely covered in soft needles. A deep green color, strong branches, and overall durability make this the perfect choice for hanging heirloom ornaments.

**Lodgepole pine (*Pinus contorta*):** Commonly spotted in western North America, the lodgepole pine gains a sculptural appearance from tufted needle growth. It gains another nickname—the twisted pine—from its unique spiraling needles.

**Slim Frasier (*Abies fraseri*):** This fir is prized for its lean shape, which makes for a dramatic statement in a small footprint. It has all the best qualities of the classic Frasier—appealing scent, strong branches, dark-blue green color, and excellent needle retention—in a wild, natural silhouette.

# Three Tree Projects for the Holiday Home

A richly decorated Christmas tree is a celebration of tradition. Families gather to hang heirloom ornaments, carefully stowed away from year to year, alongside glowing lights and twinkling tinsel. A star is placed on top and packages are tucked beneath the branches, building anticipation for Christmas Day.

The history of the decorated tree begins in Germany, when early Christmas trees were adorned with red apples—the predecessors of modern glass globes. The apples were soon paired with other edible trimmings: delicate white wafers, gingerbread, and tiny pastries in the shape of stars, angels, hearts, and flowers. Paper roses and chains, bright ribbons and tinsel, molded beeswax angels, and candles soon joined the celebratory mix, along with longer-lasting options made from metal or hand-carved wood.

The first glass ornaments appeared in the nineteenth century, when glassblowers from the German village of Lauscha began making lustrous silvered baubles. Manufactured ornaments reached U.S. shores around 1870, with nature-themed trinkets like acorns, trees, and birds quickly gaining popularity. These ornaments were soon joined by decorative stands, skirts, and electric string lights (one of Thomas Edison's many noteworthy inventions) to create the familiar, fully decorated tree that we know today.

Ornaments, lights, and other seasonal adornments have since taken on a near-endless variety of shapes, materials, and styles. The following pages showcase three of our favorite ways to dress the holiday fir, including lights, natural elements, and decorative objects—plus creative techniques for combining all of these components. (Many of the lights and decorative elements can be found at ShopTerrain.com.) Our inspiration for every look begins outdoors, as we strive to celebrate the natural world in its many forms.

# High-Country Verdigris

An inventive adaptation of classic Christmas greenery, this tree captures the majesty of nature in a rich palette of green and gold. The shapely fir was left unsheared, its naturally slender silhouette allowing ample room for decoration. Six strings of twinkle lights were carefully wrapped throughout the tree, tracing the length of each branch for an allover glow. The tall panicles (or flower stalks) of the paulownia tree serve as an unexpectedly striking accent thanks to their knobby buds and soft, golden brown hue. (Cut them after the first frost and allow them to dry, then attach them upright to the branches of the tree using floral wire.) Flowers and garlands made from stamped metal evoke luxury, while more refined elements draw inspiration from the winter garden and introduce soft, weathered tones. Gilded fresh botanicals, including burnished magnolia leaves, bridge the gap between opulent and earthy ornamentation.

**TREE**
8-foot skinny Fraser fir

**LIGHTS**
1,000-bulb LED strands

**THE DECORATIONS**

1. Fresh magnolia leaves, coated with gilding paste (see page 320)
2. Fresh seeded eucalyptus branches, dipped in gold spray paint (see page 320)
3. Preserved plumosa fern garland, painted gold
4. Dried paulownia panicles (see above)
5. Preserved moss balls
6. Verdigris oak and acorn garlands
7. Velvet ribbon
8. Golden petals ornaments
9. Copper bouquet ornaments
10. Giant glass globe ornaments
11. German clear glass ornaments
12. Hexagon facets globe ornaments

# Winter Garden

Inspired by a frost-laden landscape, this colorful tree makes a sculptural statement with bold shapes and oversize, aged metal flowers. A wild Nordmann fir is the base, with soft needles and an open-branch layout that provides space for ample decoration. Shades of blue, turquoise, and weathered gray serve as a nod to icy winter weather; the tree itself is subtly colored with a turquoise latex to match this cool palette. Building upon the wintry theme, four strands of frosted globe lights function as additional ornaments, wrapped garland-style to avoid the interior of the tree and concentrated at the tips of each major branch. (Each bulb is kept upright with a small clip at its base.) Sprays of alder and scrub pine branches are wired to the trunk of the tree at varying heights, extending outward to offer beautifully informal silhouettes, and calling to mind the wild forms of an untended garden.

**TREE**
6-foot unsheared Nordmann fir

**LIGHTS**
Frosted G40 globe lights

**THE DECORATIONS**
1. Dried blue hydrangeas
2. Preserved reindeer moss, tinted blue
3. Pinecone flowers, mounted on stakes
4. Scrub pine branches, with cones
5. Preserved oak leaves, tinted plum
6. Galvanized zinc allium stems
7. Galvanized zinc laurel branches
8. Galvanized zinc lotus flowers
9. Textured glass ornaments

# First Snow

Soft and welcoming, this tree draws color inspiration from a field of tufted grasses partially covered in snow. Clusters of foraged botanicals, including sawtooth oak leaves, dried *Allium schubertii* seed heads, and bleached protea blooms, define a palette of pure whites and muted, natural tones. The tree itself—an airy noble fir with a spartan shape—is whitewashed with a solution of diluted latex for a "snow-dusted" appearance, its trunk left untouched for a bold, vertical element. To complete this forager's tree, traditional elements are reimagined from a natural perspective: a dozen faux branches studded in tiny LED bulbs provide twinkling illumination (the lit branches are laid atop each level of noble fir boughs, with some bent double as the tree's shape tapers upward), and fillable glass globe ornaments make homes for collections of smaller natural finds. For playful texture, stems of dried and bleached bunny tail grass (*Lagurus ovatus*) are gathered into bundles, then wired to the ends of the largest branches.

**TREE**
6-foot natural noble fir

**LIGHTS**
Faux twigs topped with LED bulbs

**THE DECORATIONS**
1. Dried sawtooth oak leaves
2. Dried *Allium schubertii* seed heads
3. Dried protea flowers, bleached
4. Dried bunny tail grass, bleached
5. Metal leaves garland
6. Large white glass ornaments
7. Clear glass ornaments, filled with natural elements

# Spotlight on Winter

*rest & renewal*

———

Winter brings a hushed beauty to the world, blanketing the landscape with soft snow and glittering frost. The stillness of its cold days marks the conclusion of an old year, while its stark simplicity invites a fresh start. Holiday celebrations give way to reflective evenings beside the fireplace, planning for the seasons to come. Lush décor is replaced with clean spaces and simple greens. Outdoors, the garden too finds time for rest and renewal. Bulbs wait dormant for the earth to thaw, buds begin to form for spring's forthcoming foliage, and last year's leaves sink into the soil, enriching it for new growth to come.

Though winter weather demands a retreat indoors, cozy days at home leave ample time for contemplation of the natural world. These thoughtful moments are a gardener's respite as the days count down to spring.

## Traditions
# The Art of the Woodpile

In northern Europe, firewood is an integral part of life. Individuals across Scandinavia and Germany are uniquely dedicated to chopping, drying, and stacking their own fuel for winter fires.

This fascination with firewood no doubt has much to do with practical concerns. After all, these cold regions are known for their long winters, filled with crackling fires that need lots of wood. A single Finnish person can use a jaw-dropping 860 pounds of logs in a single year! With so much wood on hand—and a true need for heat in the depths of Nordic winters—the art of the woodpile has become a pastime for millions.

For those who stockpile their own wood, preparation for winter fires begins in spring, when the wood is cut and stacked to dry through the summer. The proper stacking method is key—and highly debated—but many people choose to build a traditional German *Holzhaufen*.

These tidy, circular piles are uniquely efficient when it comes to drying wood. They can hold lots of logs in a relatively small space and remain stable as the logs shrink and shift through the year. It's also theorized that the cylindrical form of the *Holzhaufen* helps the wood dry more quickly by drawing air into its center, creating a chimney effect via the warm interior of the stack. Best of all, its snug beehive shape makes a charming addition to the backyard.

# Midwinter Respite at Morris Arboretum Fernery

Just a short drive from downtown Philadelphia, an unusual greenhouse provides a window into Victorian horticultural history. Tucked among the gardens of the Morris Arboretum, the Dorrance H. Hamilton Fernery was built in 1899, at the height of a Victorian fern craze known as "pteridomania." After construction, arboretum founder John T. Morris ordered a collection of over five hundred plants to fill the fernery, an elegant structure of glass and steel with a gracefully curved roof. To shelter the humidity-loving specimens from Pennsylvania's cold winters, Morris turned to the latest technologies in steam heating, glass cutting, and architecture. The fernery soon became a showplace, where the era's plant lovers could explore the curious world of ferns in every season—even on the coldest January days.

During subsequent decades, the greenhouse fell into disrepair as enthusiasm for ferns faded. In 1994, the fernery was restored to its original splendor; the curved roof was refurbished, the heating system updated, and the rocky outcroppings inside rebuilt to hold lush foliage once again. Today, it's the only freestanding Victorian fernery left in North America.

Though just 53 feet long, the fernery holds countless tableaux. Ferns flourish against a miniature landscape of stony pathways, gently flowing fountains, and hidden grottos. On winter's snowiest days, it serves as a tropical escape and a unique look into garden trends of the past.

# Resources

Here is a collection of our favorite gardens and arboretums across the United States and farther afield, as well as a calendar of American flower shows; featuring incredible installations, unexpected plant specimens, and the newest tools, these shows spotlight what's new in the horticultural world and offer inspiration for the coming year.

## *Our Favorite Gardens in the United States*

**Bartram's Garden**
bartramsgarden.org
Philadelphia, PA

**Brooklyn Botanic Garden**
bbg.org
Brooklyn, NY

**The Central Garden at the Getty Center**
getty.edu/visit/center/gardens.html
Los Angeles, CA

**Chanticleer**
chanticleergarden.org
Wayne, PA

**Chicago Botanic Garden**
chicagobotanic.org
Chicago, IL

**Colonial Pennsylvania Plantation**
colonialplantation.org
Newtown Square, PA

**The Huntington Botanical Gardens**
huntington.org/gardens
San Marino, CA

**International Rose Test Garden in Washington Park**
explorewashingtonpark.org/international-rose-test-garden
Portland, OR

**Longwood Gardens**
longwoodgardens.org
Kennett Square, PA

**The Madoo Conservancy**
madoo.org
Sagaponack, NY

**The Met Cloisters**
metmuseum.org/visit/met-cloisters
New York, NY

**Mt. Cuba Center**
mtcubacenter.org
Hockessin, DE

**New York Botanical Garden**
nybg.org
Bronx, NY

**The Ruth Bancroft Garden & Nursery**
ruthbancroftgarden.org
Walnut Creek, CA

**Wave Hill**
wavehill.org
Bronx, NY

# Our Favorite Arboretums in the United States

**The Arnold Arboretum of Harvard University**
arboretum.harvard.edu
Boston, MA

**Bayard Cutting Arboretum**
bayardcuttingarboretum.com
Great River, NY

**Jenkins Arboretum & Gardens**
jenkinsarboretum.org
Devon, PA

**Morris Arboretum of the University of Pennsylvania**
morrisarboretum.org
Philadelphia, PA

**Mount Pisgah Arboretum**
mountpisgaharboretum.com
Eugene, OR

**The Scott Arboretum of Swarthmore College**
scottarboretum.org
Swarthmore, PA

**Tyler Arboretum**
tylerarboretum.org
Media, PA

# Our Favorite International Plant Destinations

**Chelsea Physic Garden**
chelseaphysicgarden.co.uk
London, UK

**Eden Project**
edenproject.com
Cornwall, UK

**Great Dixter House & Gardens**
greatdixter.co.uk
Northiam, UK

**Hortus Botanicus**
dehortus.nl
Amsterdam, Netherlands

**Insel Mainau**
mainau.de
Lake Constance, Germany

**Kew Gardens**
kew.org
London, UK

**Sissinghurst Castle Garden**
nationaltrust.org.uk/sissinghurst-castle-garden
Crankbrook, UK

**Villa d'Este**
villadestetivoli.info/storiae.htm
Tivoli, Italy

# A Calendar of Flower Shows in the United States

## February

Central Ohio Home & Garden Show
(*Columbus, OH*)

Chicagoland Home & Flower Show (*Chicago, IL*)

Cincinnati Home & Garden Show
(*Cincinnati, OH*)

Cleveland Home & Flower Show
(*Cleveland, OH*)

Colorado Garden & Home Show (*Denver, CO*)

Home & Garden Show (*Des Moines, IA*)

Jacksonville Home & Patio Show
(*Jacksonville, FL*)

Marymount Flower & Garden Show
(*Richmond, VA*)

Minnesota Home & Garden Show
(*Minneapolis, MN*)

New Jersey Flower & Garden Show
(*Somerset, NJ*)

Northwest Flower & Garden Show (*Seattle, WA*)

Portland Home & Garden Show (*Portland, OR*)

Southern Spring Show (*Charlotte, NC*)

Yard, Garden & Patio Show (*Portland, OR*)

## March

Atlanta Flower Show (*Atlanta, GA*)

Dallas Home & Garden Show (*Dallas, TX*)

Indiana Flower & Patio Show (*Indianapolis, IN*)

Kansas City Flower, Lawn & Garden Show
(*Kansas City, MO*)

Maryland Home & Flower Show
(*Timonium, MD*)

Metropolitan Louisville Home,
Garden & Flower Show (*Louisville, KY*)

New England Flower Show (*Boston, MA*)

New York Flower Show (*New York, NY*)

Philadelphia Flower Show (*Philadelphia, PA*)

Pittsburgh Home & Garden Show
(*Pittsburgh, PA*)

Southern Home & Garden Show (*Mobile, AL*)

U.S. Botanical Garden Spring Flower Show
(*Washington, DC*)

Washington Flower & Garden Show
(*Washington, DC*)

## April

Ann Arbor Flower & Garden Show
(*Saline, MI*)

San Francisco Landscape Garden Show
(*San Francisco, CA*)

St. Louis Flower Show (*St. Louis, MO*)

## August

Southern California Home & Garden Show
(*Anaheim, CA*)

# Acknowledgments

We would like to thank all those who recognize and appreciate that there is no real beauty without slight imperfection, the philosophy upon which our Terrain foundation has been built.

On the subject of foundations, thanks to our agent, Judy Linden at Stonesong, and to our team at Artisan: Lia Ronnen, Bridget Monroe Itkin, Michelle Ishay-Cohen, Jane Treuhaft, Renata Di Biase, Nancy Murray, Hanh Le, Sibylle Kazeroid, Elise Ramsbottom, Allison McGeehon, Theresa Collier, and Amy Kattan. Your tireless work helped shape the story we wanted to tell.

To the folks whose creative talents, consistent determination, and occasional grit took this book from an interesting but seemingly unattainable idea to the pages you now hold: Lacey Soslow, Melissa Bartley, Danielle Palencar, Melissa Lowrie, Caroline Lees, Laura Twilley, Matthew Muscarella, Deborah Herbertson, Kerry Ann McLean, Isa Salazar, Catherine Boggs King, and Justin Speers.

And to our Terrain family. To Richard and Meg Hayne, Wendy McDevitt, Dave Ziel, Beth Brewer, Andrew Carnie, and Denise Albright, for their enduring support, guidance, and steadfast leadership in the years since planting the original seeds of Terrain. And to all those whose daily dedication fosters our growth today: Jenny Jones, Ken George, Beth Clevenstine, Matt Bier, and the store visual teams; Matt Poarch and the field operations and receiving teams; each and every person in our home office—from the buying, merchandising, planning and allocation teams to design, web, photography, styling, and creative operations; not to mention the entire Glen Mills, Westport, Walnut Creek, Palo Alto, and Devon store teams, and our partners at Terrain Garden Cafe and Terrain Gatherings—we are truly lucky and grateful for the passion and determination every one of you brings to Terrain.

Without the creative collective experience of this incredible group, members both past and present, this book would not exist.

Here's to the next ten years. Let's keep growing.

# Index

# Photo Credits

**Page 33** Blue grama grass: Kathryn Roach/Shutterstock; ruby grass: Layue/Shutterstock; pampas grass: Lynn Whitt/Shutterstock; quaking grass: Maryna Ges/Shutterstock; tufted hair grass: LianeM/Shutterstock; Japanese forest grass: guentermanaus/Shutterstock; giant reed grass: Pelikh Alexey/Shutterstock; Mexican feather grass: Alex Sun/Shutterstock; little bluestem: beverlyjane/Shutterstock

**Page 77** Chandelier plant: topimages/Shutterstock; variegated ivy: Skyprayer2005/Shutterstock; verbena: NeCoTi/Shutterstock; jasmine: yurisyan/Shutterstock; house ivy: Myimagine/Shutterstock

**Page 193** Pat Robinson Photography

**Page 195** Vases (4): Frances Palmer and Amy Merrick

**Page 199** Clump moss: duckeesue/Shutterstock; sheet moss: Bildagentur Zoonar GmbH/Shutterstock; Spanish moss: Rob Hainer/Shutterstock; reindeer moss: Hillside Studios/Shutterstock; bottom image: Oregon Coastal Flowers

**Page 202** Anemone: studio lallka/Shutterstock; larkspur: Mariola Anna S/Shutterstock; lisianthus: AyahCin/Shutterstock; ranunculus: Natalia Van Doninck/Shutterstock; scabiosa: Debu55y/Shutterstock; hollyhock: Darrell Vonbergen/Shutterstock; English rose: Maria Rom/Shutterstock

**Page 203** Amaranth: Ole Schoener/Shutterstock; marguerite daisy: Juniors/SuperStock; mountain mint: rockerBOO/Flickr; nigella: terra incognita/Shutterstock; Queen Anne's lace: Fluke Cha/Shutterstock; sorghum: Deyana Stefanova Robova/Shutterstock; joe-pye weed: Andrey Nikitin/Shutterstock; goldenrod: Rahmi Arifah/Shutterstock; cornflower: QueSeraSera/Shutterstock; aster: Bildagentur Zoonar GmbH/Shutterstock

**Page 205** Echeveria: Ekaterina Kamenetsky/Shutterstock

**Page 217** Abbie Kiefer

**Page 221** Adam Ciccarino

**Page 222** Pat Robinson Photography

**Page 254** Flower buds: schankz/Shutterstock; leaf buds: Vira Mylyan-Monastyrska/Shutterstock

**Page 263** Muscari 'Venus': Labrynthe/Shutterstock; tulip 'Black Parrot': Taniaslonik/Shutterstock; tulip 'Lady Jane': Ole Schoener/Shutterstock; *Allium* 'Mount Everest': E. O./Shutterstock; *Allium christophii*: InfoFlowersPlants/Shutterstock; *Chionodoxa* 'Blue Giant': Bildagentur Zoonar GmbH/Shutterstock; *Narcissus* 'Apricot Whirl': Okhotnikova Ekaterina/Shutterstock; *Narcissus* 'Tête-à-Tête': Kutikan/Shutterstock; *Leucojum*: auoferten/Shutterstock; snake's head fritillaria: Eileen Kumpf/Shutterstock

**Page 335** Canaan fir: NatalieSchorr/Shutterstock; Nordmann fir: barmalini/Shutterstock